Brutally Honest
Life Management Journal

Brutally HonestLife Management Journal
A Self-Guided Journey to Achieving Success in All Areas of Your Life

Copyright © 2009 by Gregory P. LaMonaca and James H. Grim Jr

All rights reserved. No part of this book may be used or reproduced by any means, graphic, electronic, or mechanical, including photocopying, recording, taping or by any information storage retrieval system without the written permission of the publisher except in the case of brief quotations embodied in critical articles and reviews.

iUniverse books may be ordered through booksellers or by contacting:

iUniverse
1663 Liberty Drive
Bloomington, IN 47403
www.iuniverse.com
1-800-Authors (1-800-288-4677)

Because of the dynamic nature of the Internet, any Web addresses or links contained in this book may have changed since publication and may no longer be valid. The views expressed in this work are solely those of the author and do not necessarily reflect the views of the publisher, and the publisher hereby disclaims any responsibility for them.

ISBN: 978-0-5955-3436-4 (pbk)
ISBN: 978-0-5956-3623-5 (cloth)
ISBN: 978-0-5956-3494-1 (ebk)

Printed in the United States of America

iUniverse rev. date: 10.20.09

From Greg:
To Face, G, and Lis Lis, you are my world.
I love you forever and a day!

From Jim:
To Ma, who serves as my greatest mentor, to my dear wife, Cyndii, and to my two loving daughters, Meghan and Caraline.

Contents

Acknowledgments ix
Preface xi
A Note on Grammar xiii
Introduction xv
Who Are We and Why Did We Do This? xix
What Is Brutally Honest? xxi
Breakdown xxiii
A Year in a Life: Greg's Personal Journey of Life, Love, and Life's
    Many Splendid Lessons xxvii

Stage I: The Breakdown Phase 1
The Past 3
The Painful Past 9
The Pleasant Past 12
Brutally Honest Inventory 17
The Difference: Brutally Honest versus the Gurus 22
Supercharging Your Batteries 25
The Present: Brutally Honest Net-Life Statement 27
Things in Life That Charge Our Batteries 33
The Negative Drain on Our Batteries 35
Family Members Who Drain Our Batteries 36
Friends Who Drain Our Batteries 43
Work Associates Who Drain Our Batteries 49
Things in Life That Drain Our Batteries 56
Soul's Core: The Arrival 61
A Note on Discipline 64

Stage II: Creating Your Compelling Future 67
Brutally Honest Target Zones 67
Creating Brutally Honest Target Zones/A Ten-Year-Day-in-the-Life
    Statement 68
Target Zones versus Goals 72
Blasting Off to Utopia 78
Mapping: The Key to Success 89
Five-Year Target Zones 94

The Brutally Honest One-Year Zone of Excellence 115

Stage III: Quest for Utopia.. 142
Enter the Zone 144
Weekday Brutally Honest Emotional Volcano 148
Weekend Brutally Honest Emotional Volcano..............................149
Negative Emotions 151
Positive Emotions..155
Substituting Emotions..167
Your Brutally Honest Power Link 175
Your Brutally Honest Power Card..187
The Brutally Honest Daily Journal: The Final Frontier 189
Soul Mates for Life 192
About the Authors..195
Index..197

Acknowledgments

From Greg:

To my beautiful wife, Monica, who has been with me from the start and has supported me unconditionally throughout the journey. To Alyssa and Gregory, who have served as my inspiration to achieve. Thank you for your patience and willingness to listen and read through each chapter during its evolution. For an entire summer in our home in the Pocono Mountains, the process went like this: I would awake around four or five in the morning, make coffee, take a walk with Tasha, and then begin writing with Tasha at my feet. Gregory would wake around seven, come downstairs, give me a kiss, and then sit on my lap as I continued to write. Around eight, Alyssa would come down, and I would read a chapter (or they would read to me); and we would discuss the principles. Monica would then review each chapter and ultimately reviewed the entire book. As *The Brutally Honest Life Management Journal* evolved, our family did too.

To Mom and Dad for giving me the love and the foundation from which I was able to learn and grow. For Joey and Steven for showing me the ropes and standing by me. To Tasha, my beloved and most loyal friend. You provided fourteen years of unconditional love. When I lost you, I lost a piece of my soul. To Pam, as promised, your legacy lives on through the pages of this book and the inspiration, courage, and willpower that you lived your life by. To Dr. Jean Belasco, your dedication and compassion for helping children and adults alike is exceptional. To Master Michael DiPietro, you have set an example with your life and transferred innumerable traits such as courage, tenacity, persistence, character, perseverance, and dedication to me, your instructors, your students, and all those who have had the pleasure of being in your presence—no gray areas. To Jim, for your friendship and for fueling my passion to be Brutally Honest. And finally, for all of my mentors and countless authors, who have fueled my passion to learn, grow, and help others.

From Jim:

To Ma, who serves as my greatest mentor. All the good in me comes from you and your constant and never-ending love. You are always with me, watching me from heaven and telling me when to duck! To my dear wife, Cyndii, who stood by me when others did not and always said it would all work out. To my blessings from God, Meghan and Caraline, who truly taught me why I was put on this earth.

Without them, I would have never met my dear friend, Greg, and never had the chance to be Brutally Honest. To Greg, for seeing in me what at times I did not see in myself and for giving me the most precious of gifts. To Thomas D. Cooke Sr. (Ducky) for your fatherly guidance and love through many difficult years, your passing only confirmed to me how short life is. You are missed but you and the family will never be forgotten. To all those many, many people who believed in this poor kid from central Pennsylvania and took the time to fill the many voids in my life. My love and loyalty is with you always!

From Jim and Greg:

We want to thank all of our families, friends, and employees, who supported us, inspired us, and encouraged us to see this book through to fruition. Next, we want to thank our countless clients who helped form the foundation for the Brutally Honest format and techniques. To the many authors who have labored for countless hours to create many of the masterpieces that we have both utilized over the years to form the foundation of Brutally Honest, we sincerely appreciate your efforts.

Special thanks to Franklyn Frazer. We appreciate your assistance in both editing the book and utilizing the tools that it provides. You will no doubt be successful in all of your endeavours.

> *Every house where love abides and friendship is a guest is surely home, and home, sweet home; for there the heart can rest.*
> —Henry Van Dyke

Preface

The authors are not counsellors, psychologists, psychiatrists, or therapists. Thus, nothing contained within this book should be construed as rendering any medical, psychological, psychiatric, therapeutic, or similar advice. While Mr. LaMonaca is an attorney by trade, nothing in this book should be construed as rendering legal advice. This book should be used for informational purposes only and should not be relied on by the reader as rendering any professional advice. The reader is encouraged to seek out professional assistance for advice in any of the above-mentioned categories and beyond.

The information and advice published in this book or made available through the Brutally Honest Web site is not intended to replace the services of a physician or lawyer, nor does it constitute a doctor-patient or attorney-client relationship. Information in this book and on the Brutally Honest Web site is provided for informational purposes only and is not a substitute for professional medical or legal advice. You should not use any of this information for diagnosing or treating medical, psychological, or other health conditions. You should consult a physician in all matters relating to your health and particularly with respect to any symptoms that may require diagnosis or medical attention. Any action on your part in response to the information provided in this book or on the Web site is at your discretion. The authors of this book make no representations or warranties with respect to any information offered or provided on or through the Brutally Honest web site or this book. The authors of this book and the Brutally Honest companies are not liable for any direct or indirect claim, loss, or damage resulting from use of this book, the Brutally Honest Web site, and/or any Web site(s) linked to it.

A Note on Grammar

In creating this product, we have completed countless revisions over many months and years. Once we created what we believed to be the final version, there soon came another final version, followed by the absolute final version, which was eclipsed by yet another update. As many of you who have followed this journey over the years know, we have professed to be within days of publishing this book for a long time. Once we had it to a point where we were ready to move to the next level and get the book ready for publishing, we sought out the help of several individuals, including Franklyn Frazer to whom we owe many thanks for his editing skills. After he was done, he took a lawyer and a salon owner's writings and gave them author's validity. We then circulated it among several other individuals to review. In every case, there were ongoing comments about suggested grammar, spelling, and style changes, some of which contradicted each other. We then continued to incorporate some of the changes, only to find them followed by additional changes. In the end, we took a step back and decided to decide. We took our own advice and decided to release the book.

While many of the initial readers have lauded the book's style and content, we don't expect to win any Pulitzer prizes or go down in the writer's hall of fame. Quite frankly—we're being Brutally Honest—the book you have in front of you is not about the writing style but about the power behind the words. While it is not our desire to have you find grammar and spelling mistakes, to the extent you do find some mistakes or simply things you don't agree with, that is okay, as it will mean that you have read through the entire book and absorbed its meaning. Like life, this book is also not perfect. It does contain, however, the blood, sweat, tears, and passion that fueled us both. In all sincerity, the book you hold in your hands is the result of countless years of thought that is designed to change the lives of those who choose to take the journey. We expect—and welcome—spirited debate and questions. It is our hope that you get out of it as much joy as we had in writing it.

Introduction

Why keep a journal? With everything you do, how will you ever find the time to keep a journal? You will *make* the time. Why? Because you know it will increase your odds of attaining what you set out to achieve. Statistically, individuals who write down their goals are more likely to achieve them. Writing down your thoughts and feelings is also a way of memorializing them for future reference, as well as for future generations, should you choose to share them. My partner and I have been keeping journals for many years, through good times and bad. When times seem bleak,

> *The chains of habit are generally too small to be felt until they are too strong to be broken.*
> —Samuel Johnson

we have referred to past entries in our journals made during periods when we had similar problems, and we reviewed how we overcame those situations. I promise you this: *The Brutally Honest Life Management Journal* will be like no journal you have ever seen, used, or heard of. Using this journal will be life-transforming. This journal is *yours*. No one will grade it, and no one will see it (unless you choose). You can use it however you want. If you choose to participate in all of the exercises—great. If you choose to do only some, that's fine too. You get out what you put in. Your willingness to read this and do the exercises says a lot about you. Whatever stage of life you are in, you will benefit greatly from completing the exercises and capturing your thoughts in the pages of this journal. If you fill a glass halfway with water, you can only get half a glass to drink. If, however, you pour enough water to fill the glass to the top, you will get a full glass to drink. If you not only fill the glass to the top, but continue to add water, it will overflow with abundance. By completing all of the exercises in this journal and carrying forward the lessons you will learn along the way, your own personal life will overflow with abundance.

As the authors of this ground-breaking system, we know this: many of you will fail. You will find the exercises too tough or too time-consuming, and you will concoct many excuses for not following through. We also know many of you will feel that, while the information may be useful, you already have all the answers. If you feel that this applies to you, we would ask you to honestly assess all areas of your life. Are you truly perfect? Are there really *no* areas of your life that can be improved? Do you really have all of the answers to life's mysteries? Remember as you read this that you are alone. You have only yourself to answer to. Maybe if you allow yourself to be fully engaged in the following pages you will find yourself confronting questions that have lain dormant for many years. You might even say that you don't need to write any answers down because you are able to keep everything in your head. But remember that the excuses we make in life are ours and ours alone.

That said, we are also abundantly aware of this: if you have what it takes to fully commit to the Brutally Honest system and give yourself the gift of full immersion into the activities and exercises that follow, your life will be catapulted to a level that only a few individuals ever reach. Like everything else in life that is good, the exercises that follow will take effort and enthusiasm and will often take you to parts of your past that are painful; they may bring out repressed feelings that you have long since forgotten. This is not a book to bring to the beach to read casually in an attempt to displace reality. If that's what you want, put this down and go out and get a *Harry Potter* or *Twilight* book.

When Thomas Edison tried inventing the light bulb, he failed thousands of times, but he looked at each failure as another way not to invent the light bulb. Thomas Edison didn't fear failure because he knew that each failure was taking him one step closer to his goal. What if Bill Gates and Paul Allen had decided to stay enrolled in Harvard and not drop out to pursue their grand vision? What will your life be like if you don't follow through with all of the exercises in this journal? More important, ask yourself this: "What will my life be like when I complete all of the exercises within this book?" Having just started on your journey, you may not be able to answer that question yet. Having lived the Brutally Honest System and lifestyle and having seen countless individuals radically transform their lives in amazing and abundant ways, we can tell you unconditionally that the individuals who take the leap with us and fully immerse themselves in the activities, answering all of the questions completely and honestly, will take themselves to new heights that are only realized by a few.

We have seen the value of these journals in our own lives as well. For example, once a year, Greg pulls out the journal he first completed when he was beginning in business. He looks through the various goals that he set and is amazed at how far he has come. He recognizes his accomplishments, as well as his failures. As he evolves through life's mazes and obstacles, he often refers to that original journal for inspiration. Over the years, he has been able to reflect on what it was he wanted to achieve and determine whether he was on track or not. If he was off course, he would map out a plan to get back on track. At times, he saw that some of his goals were either impractical or no longer part of his ultimate vision. Having a written record of his life gave him the ability to make corrections in a proactive manner and gain control of his destiny. Since that original journal, many years ago, Greg has made countless entries in his journals, set new, loftier goals, and evaluated where his life has been, where he is, and where he wants to head.

The point is that no one can remember everything. No matter how bright you are and how vivid an existing thought may be, it too shall pass. By capturing your thoughts in writing in this journal and in your Brutally Honest daily journal, you will have an outlet, a place to ensure that you will not forget, and a place to create and track your life plan by way of your Brutally Honest Target Zones.

By completing the following exercises, you are setting yourself apart from most people in the world who choose not to do so. The success rate of individuals who truly embrace and complete these exercises dwarfs that of the rest of the world, the people who choose to simply meander through each day doing only the things that are necessary to simply get by. These people jump onto rafts and head down the rapids with blindfolds on, having no idea where they will wind up. On the other hand, by participating in a Brutally Honest lifestyle and completing this life management journal, you will learn how to carefully choose the right raft, find the best paddles, and map out and traverse the river. You also have the best helmet and protective gear to keep you safe when life's inevitable rapids throw you into the water. Through the skills and lessons contained within this life management journal, you will be able to immediately get back onto the raft and head toward your destination.

> *In a legendary study in 1953, Yale University asked students in its graduating class what their goals were and discovered that only 3 percent had any written goals. Twenty years later, Yale surveyed that same class and found that the 3 percent who had written their goals had earned more money than the other 97 percent combined.*

As this book is being released, our country is going through one of the most catastrophic economic times in history since the Great Depression. Unemployment is at historic levels; families are losing fortunes; retirement savings are being obliterated; and foreclosures are at record highs, leaving countless individuals homeless and forcing retirees to try to find jobs to survive. What was thought to be the standard path to achieving the American dream was shattered overnight. We are living in unprecedented times that have forced us to reevaluate every area of our lives. Those individuals that thought they had all the answers have found out that they are in need of new thought patterns.

Choose *now* to create excellence. Commit to yourself today to creating a never-ending flow of water that overflows your glass of life. Let's begin *your* journey to Utopia. The hottest trend right now is reality television. It seems that every new television show coming out is about someone's life. Why are we so consumed with this type of entertainment? Because it's nice to see others making mistakes we believed were only happening to us. We also enjoy seeing the lives of our heroes unfolding in front of us. Do you realize that, as you are reading these words, your life is also evolving in the ultimate reality show, entitled "My Life?" You are the producer, director, writer, and star of the show. You have full power and discretion to write the script for the rest of your life. If the rest of the world were to view this Emmy-winning program, what would you want it to show and reflect about you? As you work through this journal, keep this in mind: with each decision you make in life, you are creating your own reality show. Unlike real television, however, you can't go back and redo a scene, yell "Cut!", or edit out things you don't like. You can, however, design the ultimate show. Let's get started!

> *I keep six honest serving men (They taught me all I know); their names are What and Why and When and How and Where and Who.*
> --Rudyard Kipling

Who Are We and Why Did We Do This?

Why we did this is an easy question to answer. The simple, Brutally Honest truth is that we both believe that if you do not mentor and help others, then the gift that God has given you stops. Despite our diverse and varied backgrounds, what has been paramount to each of us is helping as many people as possible achieve their hopes, dreams, and goals and imparting in them the passion and desire to go forth and to help as many people as they can, thereby insuring an ongoing ripple effect, which will expand exponentially into infinity.

Now the question of who we are is a bit more difficult to explain. A lawyer and a salon owner may not seem like a likely pairing to team up on a book on how to succeed in all areas of life. But, as the cliché goes, you can't judge a book by its cover. No better words can describe the relationship and appearances of the authors. We are undoubtedly two very different personalities: Greg comes from a large and loving Italian family, and Jim comes from a fragmented household where his wonderful mother died early and his father took off to "find himself." Greg is in constant contact with his parents and brothers, and Jim does not know where his sisters are.

Over the years, despite our initial differences, we discovered that we shared countless things in common, the core of this similarity being our unwavering belief in family, faith, and loyalty and an almost obsessive desire to help others. The ability to face and deal with adversity, to hold tight and let go, to think deeply and be whimsical, to plan a safe voyage step by step and plunge down the face of a wave all combined to forge the phenomenal friendship that has formed the backdrop of this book. We spent many hours together in a legal forum and through these countless hours of hearings and counseling, our stories began to unfold and our friendship deepened. Neither one of us had a silver-spoon life, and both of us had to overcome much adversity to get where we are today; however, both of us have consistently kept journals of our lives, and from those journals we were able to *learn* from our pasts and *plan* for our futures. Please remember that if your life is worth living, then it is worth recording.

Like a fine wine that has come of age, it is now time to tell our stories to the world. It is time to tell the world the straightforward, Brutally Honest principles that shaped our lives and brought us success. It is time to continue the Brutally Honest cycle and give to others so that the process can regenerate and continue. This may sound a bit out there to you right now, but—believe us—when you finish the journal you will understand the power of the statement.

Today we begin an odyssey that will transcend everything that you have ever known. The very fact that you have purchased the book and had the courage to begin to read it humbles us. You have taken a huge step forward in your life, and we want you to take a moment before you go any further. Read the following passage out loud:

> *Today my life begins again. All the things that I have done or not done in the past are wiped clean, and I begin to control my life. I will live by my standards and not society's. I control my thoughts and actions. Through my desire to better myself each and every day, I am building my Brutally Honest path to success."…Jim Grim*

What we have to give you is a gift that can only be realized by giving it to yourself and others. The gift we have to give is an intricate program that will reintroduce you to the wonderful person you knew many, many years ago, during a time when life was simple and your vision was clear.

By purchasing this book, you have already begun to live your life in a Brutally Honest way. You have decided that no matter how intimidating this book may seem, you will not settle for less than all that life has to offer. You are invited to take part in the most revolutionary, earth-shattering program ever shared with the world. If you take this challenge, one thing is for sure: your life will never be the same. The technologies and techniques about which you will read are the cumulative effort of our never-ending journey to be better and help others better themselves. Thank you for allowing us the privilege to help you, for it is in the helping of others that our destiny is shaped. We invite you to join us on a journey that will help you find true happiness and self-fulfillment.

> *"It is through our failures that success seeds are planted. It is through the recognition of and learning from our failures that these seeds are fertilized, and it is through the willingness to take corrective, future actions that abundant trees reign free."… Gregory LaMonaca*

What Is Brutally Honest?

The Brutally Honest system is the sum of the authors' life experiences, work, passion, and the obstacles we have overcome. We designed a system to combat the type of failure experienced with mainstream self-help products. Brutally Honest consists of a revolutionary three-step process. As you work your way through this journal, you will also work your way through the three Brutally Honest steps.

In the first step, you will begin by narrowing in on, defining, and creating a crystal-clear picture of what it is *you* need—*not* what society says you need. This is the critical difference, what has transformed the lives of the authors' countless clients, family members, and friends.

Step one, the Breakdown Phase, will lead you through an intense yet magical journey into the deepest reaches of your being, where you will ultimately reach your Soul's Core. It is at this magical and illusive place where individuals are finally alone with their thoughts, where stereotypes don't exist, peer pressure is gone, and guilt, marketing, and social pressures all disappear. Through this descent, you will seek out and find your Soul. Your Soul will then be your guide, your partner, and your unconditional friend and mentor.

Only once you arrive at Soul's Core will you be ready to develop *your* individual and personal Brutally Honest Target Zones®. Target Zones are your personalized goals, which form figurative targets that you seek out, aim for, and unite with. Once you are at the Soul's Core, the Brutally Honest system moves into overdrive in assisting you to clearly define *your* Brutally Honest Life Management Systems®. Stage two of the Brutally Honest system, unlike most self-help programs, incorporates all areas of your life and transcends to your family, friends, and associates by way of the positive energy that emanates from them. The Brutally Honest system is designed not only to be implemented by you but also to impact anyone else with whom you choose to share your newfound gifts.

Most programs find one family member attending an all-day or weekend seminar and coming home hyped-up and motivated. His or her family, however, not having gone through the same experience, is not able to fully appreciate what that person went through and doesn't experience the same feelings. The authors have determined that one key component to creating a fulfilling life is the unity of the family. Using the Brutally Honest system generates true communication, perhaps for the first time in years, and families are reunited in a common goal.

Lastly, once the life plan is solidified, step three, the journey to Utopia, begins.

This journey to Utopia is an ongoing process to not only reach the goals set in one's Brutally Honest Life Plan but also to learn the critical skills of self-evaluation as the journey unfolds. Most programs teach one how to set and achieve goals. While this is admirable, the reality is that no plan can be left unchecked. In the process of transcending through the Brutally Honest Life Plan, you will be taught how to define, evaluate, re-evaluate, and continue to improve your life.

Most self-help systems end with the individual attempting to achieve his or her predetermined goals. We recognized, after years of practice and teaching, that things change in the real world—and change quickly. With the Brutally Honest program you are about to embark on, you will learn the skill of adaptation and develop the mind frame to react quickly to life's curveballs. You will be ready and able to spread the word to others. One of the most rewarding activities we can do is to mentor others and make a real difference in someone's life. Frankly, that is the reason Brutally Honest exists.

> *Utopia is the never-ending pursuit of excellence measured by the satisfaction of living life to the fullest.*
> —Gregory LaMonaca

By undertaking the exercises throughout this journal and recording and writing down your answers, you will be able to measure where you have been, where you are presently, and where you want to go. This self-analysis forms the basis of Brutally Honest. Let's begin our journey with your personal Breakdown.

Breakdown

Here we go! Put your seatbelts on and get ready for the rest of your life.

Most self-help programs on the market look great, are colorful, and make amazing claims to help people do everything—end depression, lose tons of weight overnight, make millions of dollars—you name it. While the claims are often found to be true for that author, unless you can match apples to apples and compare all of the author's criteria with those of the reader, the reader is often left with the empty feeling of having read about how the author achieved amazing results, while being unable to even come close to achieving the same results. Why is this? Quite simply, what works for one person who may be a trust fund baby with no job, living in their beach house on the West coast, does not necessarily work for a single mother of five, working two jobs to feed her children. Seeing this significant gap in many other self-help programs, the authors developed the Brutally Honest system to combat this discrepancy, by allowing each individual to clearly define what it is he or she needs and *not* simply promoting what we think that person needs.

When you reach the inevitable end of your life, and you look back, you will not get a second chance. This is certain. We also know something else to be certain, however; you have a second chance *now*. Please do not wait until it is too late to change your destiny. Being Brutally Honest will truly transform your life. It will transform your way of thinking!

Let's look at some traditional, mainstream self-help programs geared to address people's concerns, fears, or issues in any number of areas: weight loss, depression, financial difficulty, phobias, and illnesses. Individuals are attracted initially to some promise made by the author to help out their situation. Someone who is overweight will naturally be hooked by the promise to lose massive amounts of weight overnight by following an author's teachings. Fueled by the promise of losing the weight, that person runs to the store to buy the book. He gets to the weight loss section of the bookstore, and sure enough, right in front of him is the alluring multicolored book, *Lose Fifty Pounds Overnight*. If he was excited going into the store, he is now on a new high. He scans through the first few pages in the store before buying the book. On the way home, he fantasizes about how his life is going to be when he loses all that weight.

When he gets home, he immediately dives into the book where he finds time slipping away as he moves from chapter to chapter. There is no doubt that the book has captured his attention, perhaps the first time a book has done so in a while. As is most often the case, the contents of this book are, in fact, accurate and the author's claims can be validated. The critical difference is whether the results achieved by the author will work for the person who is reading the book. If the book's method's can be utilized by others, would it take a strict, exact duplication of the author's experience and process, under the exact circumstances that the methods worked for the author?

In our example, the man begins to do the things that the author did. Initially, he even finds results. However, as is the case more often than not, because his circumstance, body type, available exercise machines, ability to exercise, health conditions, metabolism, family commitments, and the like are different from the author's, the results are short-lived and yield little or no long-term results. The man then gets caught up in the cycle of buying product after product based upon the newest author's claims to have the magic pill that will once and for all make a difference.

Before you figure out where you want to go, you must first determine where you are. One of Greg's favorite places in his youth and adult life has always been Disneyland, one of the most magical places on earth. He has been there with his parents and brothers growing up, on his honeymoon, and later with his family. It's a place where a person can temporarily suspend reality and embark on a magical trip where life's other pressures seem to dissolve. Despite having been there many times, he can never wait to go again.

Greg has lived on the East Coast all his life. Should he decide to go to Disneyland again, despite having been there several times before, he would have difficulty getting there without help of some type. If he packed his car and begin driving, while he might begin to go in the right direction, he would inevitably get lost. Visions of Disneyland are like our goals. Without your having a plan and a map, your goals will remain unfulfilled and unrealized dreams, no matter how amazing and vivid they may be.

What do you dream of?
- A large family?
- A great marriage?
- A quest to help those less fortunate than you?
- Peace and solitude?
- A long, healthy life?

> *That happy state of mind, so rarely possessed, in which we can say, "I have enough," is the highest attainment of philosophy. Happiness consists, not in possessing much, but in being content with what we possess. He who wants little always has enough.*
> —Johann George Zimmerman

- Incredible wealth and prosperity?
- A mansion overlooking the Pacific Ocean?
- A fulfilling career?
- More certainty?
- Investment properties?
- Weight loss?
- Better health?
- Less fear in your life?
- More happiness?
- More free time to pursue your passions?

There are an infinite number of possibilities to pursue. We will guide you through the process of defining and visualizing *your* dreams and will assist you in developing *your* Brutally Honest Target Zones in later chapters. Initially, you must review your past to help determine where you are and how you got there. While, in the words of Anthony Robbins, "the past doesn't equal the future," it can be a great tool in helping you determine how you got where you are.

A Year in a Life:
Greg's Personal Journey of Life, Love, and Life's Many Splendid Lessons

At age fourteen, a time when most children are dealing with typical teenage issues like dating, acne, beginning high school, and a menagerie of other milestones, I was blessed—yes, blessed—with a diagnosis that has afforded me a life of lessons that have shaped my character, personality, drive, and being. While initially characterized as an enemy that invaded my body, over the years this enemy became an ally that I have embraced and vowed never to let overcome me. I have chosen to have it assist me, teach me, and guide me. Benign tumors, throughout many areas of my body, would debilitate me at times, causing me to be unable to walk or lift my arms. I experienced multiple bouts of radiation therapy; severe lethargy; thousands of hours in hospitals; hundreds of different doctor visits; innumerable hospital stays all over the East coast; tens of thousands of X-rays, MRIs, CT scans, myelograms, bone scans, blood tests, pokes, and prods; multiple periods of disability; multiple surgeries; and a traveling army of pain that would cripple me at times. All this created an inverse effect on my brain, as it strengthened my resiliency and determination. Through my well-documented medical journey I may be able to help other children someday who are afflicted with a similar condition, as I am the test case for future generations and have been written up in medical journals.

They say that the mind represses those things that would cause pain if revealed. In the pages that follow, I reveal to you a year of my personal journal in an effort to show firsthand how I have used my journal to capture, learn from, grow, and permanently memorialize significant life events that have shaped who I am. With minor exceptions, what follows are exact excerpts from my actual journal. As such, while some sections may appear repetitive or disjointed, I have left them that way for accuracy and accountability. While most entries were written on the date referenced, some of the entries were written after the fact out of necessity. Keep in mind that your journal is *your* journal. There is no correct format. Use the following as a guide only. It is with extreme reverence and respect that I share these pages with you.

January 16, 2005
Unfortunately, I start by describing my health, as it is one of the most pressing issues as I write. In November, while playing with Gregory, I injured my mid back (T-12). As I went

to pick him up, I crashed to the ground as it felt like someone struck my mid spine with an axe, causing me to collapse like a deck of cards as it doubled me over. This was the same day as Alyssa's Xmas dance recital in Delaware at the Wilmington Playhouse. In fact it was about two hours before time. I literally crawled upstairs, hoisted myself over and into the tub, ran the water as hot as it could go and allowed the scorching water to hit my skin. Despite the unfortunate start to the day, with Monica's assistance and two walking sticks, the day ended in wonder as I watched Alyssa put on the show of her life on center stage. As always, she brought me to tears. I couldn't have been prouder of her.

As the weeks went on, the pain continued to worsen and began to spread to other areas of my body, including my lower back and hips. I originally went to Doctor Bongiovanni "Bongi" (my primary, general practitioner Doctor) in conjunction with a neurologist. The pain was unbearable. (on a 0–100 scale of pain with 100 being the most unbearable, excruciating pain imaginable), my pain would fluctuate from a 90 to a 70. I have been dealing with pain since age 14 and have routinely rejected any types of pain medicine contrary to my Doctors advice except in exceptional circumstances as I trained my mind to withstand unbearable amounts of pain. My pain tolerance has been hardened over the years and normally can withstand unbearable amounts of pain. Here however, my mind could not withstand the onslaught that I was being dealt. Nothing seemed to work. Medicine failed to help, rest didn't work as I lay twisting and turning praying and hoping to find some position that would alleviate the surges.

Thankfully I went to see Bongi again who made me get a CT scan as a precaution because my thighs had begun to develop shooting pains that felt like electricity shooting through them. Sometimes you have to ask yourself whether you are just lucky or whether there are other forces above guiding the course of life. Of course I believe that God was/is watching out for me. Why in the world would I go to my GP Doctor for something like this? Why Bongi? Why would he ask all the right questions and convince me to go get the Ct scan? I trusted Bongi as he is one of the few genuine Doctors around who takes the time to help because he really cares. I should have known something was seriously wrong. I went from doing leg extensions with hundreds of pounds to barely being able to lift the bar in a matter of weeks. The CT scan showed my disease (hemangiomatosis) got worse in both T-12 which was impinging on the spinal cord as well as my lower back. In essence, my x-ray of my lower back consisted of tumors everywhere which eroded the joint space between the hip socket and the hip causing the protective fluid to be gone, hence, bone on excruciating bone. I went home and looked up T-12 on the computer to see how this impingement on the spinal cord affects someone. I saw that this area affects the leg muscles neurologically. The lights went on. This is what was causing the leg pain. At this time, I *also realized just how much my legs had weakened. When I would bend down and my knees started to bend, my legs would give out, ie: if I am on the ground in the middle of the room with nothing to grab on to, I cannot stand up with leg strength alone and would be stranded indefinitely without assistance. I am quickly becoming paralyzed!*

Since then, I have been back to the neurologist for an EMG (I passed), and one of the Worlds best Tumor specialists in Philadelphia. He had the films reviewed by his radiologist over the holidays. The results were that the tumor had gotten worse. He sent me to see a spine surgeon on an expedited basis. We discussed surgical options. He sent me however for additional tests (Ct scans/MRI). I am meeting with Dr. Jean Belasco next week. She is one of the nations top pediatric oncologists at the Children's Hospital of Philadelphia who has been my Doctor since age 14 and remains so due to the rarity of my condition. She can do no wrong in my eyes. I trust her unconditionally, and despite her very well reasoned recommendation for me to see an adult Dr., as she is a pediatric oncologist, she still has been the one that has been there from day one. She said we could explore the newer generation medications such as interferon (NOTE: I was on this years ago) plus others. Also radiation has <u>always</u> worked before, despite the inherent risk with those approaches, they are a lot less invasive that surgery. We will see what life holds in the future.

Despite the curse that lies ahead, the true test of a man or woman's character lies in the lessons he/she learns during the journey. It can always be worse. Life affords me the ultimate opportunity to learn from everything in my path. There is no benefit, or purpose in wallowing in self pity. Who am I to complain when scores of others suffer so much more than I? My purpose is to empower and encourage others. If I can inspire others by my attitude, then I continue to serve out God's plan for me. This is why <u>LIFE IS GREAT!!!</u> I try to adjust my inner frame of reference to laugh when I feel pain and cry when I am happy. The journal helps because as I read back, I can see that while in prior years, I had significant pain flair ups, I could read in July of last year that I felt awesome!! It is clear however that I must plan forward to anticipate health issues.

February 7, 2005

Ok, here's the scoop. As indicated previously, my condition has gotten worse in two key areas: 1) entire lower back and 2) T-11.

At T-11, it is now further impinging on the spinal cord which hampers my ability to stand up, sit down and walk up and down stairs. How vulnerable I feel. All the knowledge, studying, bodybuilding, martial arts, money and notoriety cannot help me walk! I will be getting radiation therapy in 2-3 weeks. It worked before, and I hope and pray it will work again. As has been the case in the past, the doctors do not want me to lift weights. While this is prudent medical advice, since day 1, lifting weights, martial arts and exercise have been the things physically that helped me overcome while my upper body strength allows me to hoist myself up and down right now and mentally keeps me focused.

My body may be weaker, I may be more tired, it takes me forever to get dressed and get around but my mind is sharper than ever. My passion is high, my determination is unyielding and I will get through this obstacle God has given me to overcome. I do truly feel very lucky to be alive; married to the most incredibly beautiful woman God could have given me, who gave me two Great Kids!! My parents, friends are a great support and I am living out my dreams. Life is not perfect. While the pain is incredible at times (a 100,000 on a 1–10 scale), It's ok. It could always be worse. I can deal with the pain and I will overcome this and if it does not lessen, and gets worse, well, my desire, passion and strength will also be increased. If I give in, or seek pity, it serves no purpose. I will move on and learn how to overcome every obstacle placed in my way!!

March 3, 2005

OK, where do I begin? As always, I begin by being thankful for everything I have, for all of the great gifts I have been given and for all of my sincere thanks to God for all of the blessings he has given me. While my physical health is getting worse, my mental strength and attitude is at an all time high.

Physically, from my knees down are totally numb and tingly. I still cannot stand up or sit down without assistance from my upper body or walking sticks. I have completed week one of two weeks of radiation therapy. What wonderful people the technicians are. I actually feel guilty because all of the other patients in this unit are suffering from cancer and the unit is called the "cancer center". Each day as I get done my treatments, I look at the poster hanging up in the lobby of young, cancer patients with big smiles. How terrible it is that these amazing kids have to be inflicted with this before they can fully enjoy life. I look each day at their smiling faces so I don't forget them. My low back pain is between a 7–9 each day and is very sharp. It feels as if I put a wet finger into a light socket. The pain is jolting and excruciating at times. My thighs burn and my legs get weaker by the day. Going up and down steps is mentally and physically draining. I look like a seal as I migrate each step on my stomach, head first, using my upper body strength to drag my lower body up one step at a time, taking me aprox 5–10 minutes to get up the stairs.

I started on an experimental, tumor reducing drug, called thalitomide (the same drug that caused birth defects yeas ago and was taken off the market. It was reintroduced for its potential to treat tumors). These things kick the shit out of me making me very tired. I also started to get vertigo (where the bed felt like it was spinning out of control). I had a *precautionary MRI of the brain and thankfully it was negative. The good news is they did find a brain. Lol. The vertigo went away.*

It's funny that for years I have been studying and researching individuals that overcame obstacles. People have always told me that I filled these roles as well. I never accepted that. I do feel now that through my suffering I gain strength. I won't accept pity. It is in times of struggle that one gains character. There are things I can control and things I cannot. God has plans for me and I know whatever the outcome, it will be just. This I cannot control. I can control however how I react to each challenge. As long as my mind is alive, I will rise up to any challenge. I learned to change my "state". Instead of crying when the "lightning bolt jolts" surge through me, I laugh. If I stumble, I get up. People tell me how bad they feel for me. I tell them that there is no reason to feel bad or sorry for me. I tell them how lucky I am. I have been dealing with this since age 14. This is all I know, my "norm". While this disease pervades me, it also strengthens me. Through my progression, I hopefully will create research to help others who may be inflicted with the same thing. I am told that I still am the only person in the world with this condition.

You also learn during times like this who your true, "inner circle" is. Of course everyone asks how you are. These are people in the outer circle, caring, well intentioned friends but who move on with their lives. As you get closer to your inner core you find your true "soul" partners. Monica is of course the inner core. She is totally immersed with compassion, love and always places her needs last to me and the kids. She is my role model. "Liss" and "G", god bless them. They are helping out and are by my side tending to my needs. Certain friends go out of their way to help for no other reason than they care and want to help. They don't do it to look good or gain credit. Pure selflessness. My Family, Mom, Dad, Steven and Joey are the same.

I get a chance now to "walk the walk". <u>As we speak there is a race going on with the hope that radiation at T-11 shrinks the tumor before the tumor progresses where I would need surgery.</u> Either way I will survive and dedicate my life to helping others achieve their dreams and being the best Husband possible to Monica and a great role model to Alyssa and Gregory. I've learned to thank others for their influence on my life. Too often, we try to look cool and put on tough faces. All that does is cause unnecessary stress. We must enjoy life and stop the petty BS.

March 5, 2005

Today was somewhat amazing. It is a Saturday and I woke up in a complete stupor around 7:30 from the two Thalitomide I took right before bed around 11:30. I nonetheless got dressed and went to work. I was there all day till 4:30. My legs felt very heavy and numb from the knees down. I fell once in the office, thankfully right next to the couch. That night we went to church, then the bookstore then home.

What I realized was that my lower back, while still hurting, was <u>better</u> than 2 days earlier. If it was an 8–9 then, now it was a 6–7. I also felt very good before going to bed tonight. While these might be small changes, they are the first positive changes in a long time. I will nonetheless savor each small victory.

My attitude is great, I have committed to wanting to help at least 1 million people achieve their dreams<u>, or at least leave them in a better position for having met me</u>. I am on my way.

March 7, 2005 *"D Day"*

Today saw a whirlwind of emotion. I went today to meet a neurosurgeon at HUP. He said that I am a candidate for surgery at T-11 but not on the low back as the tumors are too widespread there whereby an operation could find me easily bleeding to death. Surgery would consist of removing the affected bone and replacing it with another which would be grafted from my own thigh bone and that of a cadaver. 7 days in the hospital, 6 weeks at home and 2–3 months recovery. He suggests doing it in the near future but believes it is ok to see if the radiation works.

Radiation therapy ends tomorrow. As such, I am now in a race to see if the radiation therapy will work before my leg weakness gets completely debilitating. My legs are getting weaker each day and are numb from the knees down. Getting up and down stairs, and in and out of cars are very difficult. Pain in my lower back has gotten a little better probably because of the steroids the Doctor's put me on, thalidomide, or both.

It would be every easy to feel sorry for myself, depressed or have others take pity on me. That is not me. That is not how I choose to live. I will overcome this regardless what direction God chooses. Either way, I commit each day to inspire others, be a role model to my family and to increase my learning process as I build character.

I commit to control only those things that I can fully control such as my attitude. So many others suffer far more than I and have not had the incredible life that I have.

It felt nice today taking out the Porsche and opening it up with the top down. It is my alter ego and provides the speed and adrenaline I currently lack. Unfortunately, they are calling for more snow this week.

It's amazing how the body works. At all stages of my life, any injury or weakness I had in one part was compensated by strength in others. Clearly, my upper body strength and triceps are the reason I am currently getting by as they hoist my lower body up and down.

This has also helped me perfect my skills as a lawyer, a motivator and a person. I am *truly on top of my game as I am called on daily to help my clients and have the power to make them sleep better at night knowing they have someone in their corner. Jim and I are moving rapidly with Brutally Honest. All of these lessons will hopefully grace the pages of one or more Brutally Honest books. Nothing in life is a crisis. Each challenge, no matter how big, is another opportunity to elevate you to the next level.*

I am prepared for either the option to heal through God's will or for surgery. If surgery is the course, I will use the down time to write, develop and put together marketing plans for when I am better. No doubt I will be on an emotional roller coaster, but I've designed the car, I'm learning the curves and the track and will ride it on my journey to improve. Thank you God! Life is great!

It's very important for me to instill all the right traits in Alyssa and Gregory. They are two wonderful, active children who make Monica and me proud. It is a joy seeing them absorb all of life's lessons. They adore reading thanks to Monica and love to learn about finances. It is my goal to insure that they are both self sufficient and will not have to rely on others to achieve and accomplish their life's goals. They are also very well mannered which is absolutely required. In the end, it will be up to them. Now however, we will try to give them the benefits of our own mistakes and life's lessons. Along with Monica, I love them all with every ounce of my heart. We are a "family" and stick together through good times and bad.

March 18, 2005

It looks like the figurative race is coming to an end. Over the last 2 weeks my weakness has significantly increased in my thighs. Going up/down stairs is almost impossible and scares the hell out of me. A couple of court appearances were difficult getting around.

<u>I called the neurosurgeon today to schedule the operation.</u> *The fact is however that I am mentally prepared to move forward. At the rate I am going, I can't continue to wait to see if radiation will work. I know there is a master plan and reason for everything and I accept this as just another piece of my learning curve in life. Each day I grow mentally stronger. This has provided me with an excellent opportunity to speak with Alyssa and Gregory about overcoming obstacles and focusing on the things you can control while not dwelling on the things you can't.*

Monica as always has inspired me as well. I know how much she hurts inside and wants to take my pain away, yet she tries to be strong on the outside in front of me. She has gone above and beyond in helping me.

I have spent a lot of time writing the Brutally Honest book. I have incorporated all my years of study and research in the area of personal success into the book in addition to a myriad of various psychological, philosophical and NLP aspects. Jim is working on the business aspect while I'm doing this. Monica and I went out again this week to create the "LaMonaca Life Management plan" using the Brutally Honest system as a framework. We discussed a lot of things and it went very well. Monica is off next week (Spring break) and will meet with Linda (our CPA) to move forward with the plan.

All else is well. Low back pain has eased. LIFE IS GREAT!

<u>March 20, 2005</u> *"Decision day"*

It looks as though surgery is imminent. Yesterday found me getting up early and going into the office. I could barely get up the steps and had to throw my bag up each step.

I left and went to lunch (Sushi) with Chris and Howard. I then took the Porsche out for a drive with the top down and back to the house for a Jacuzzi.

When I was taking my shower and toweling off in the bathroom in my downstairs office, I fell backwards, collapsing down and back smashing my head into the floor as my lower body could not support my upper body with the slightest bend in my knee. As I laid there alone on the shower floor with blood flowing from my head, **I saw the decision quite clear. Enough was enough.** Monica came in to help me up. My head had a nice lump and was cut. I could only laugh as I perceived what has happened to my body. Since age 14, I have spent thousands of hours in the Gym and Dojo. Now, to watch my lower half fade away is difficult. On the other hand, my upper body strength has afforded me the opportunity to exist, get up and move.

Once I was up and dressed, instead of going to the Emergency Room, I wanted, and needed, to go to church, which we did. Dad arranged for someone to come and give me communion in the crying room where we were all seated. That night we all played "Cash flow" till 3:00 am. It was fun and educational.

Once done, I could feel that my legs were worse. I tried crawling backwards up the steps. Although I ultimately made it, it was exhausting. **My life on the upstairs, and perhaps everywhere, is now on pause.** That said, I need to focus on moving forward, getting better and not backwards.

With work, I can arrange to meet people in the downstairs conference room and use the laptop. All cases need to be reassigned.

I will call the Doctor today to let him know the exigency of my situation. I am confident that everything will work out fine. You plan for events like this. I believe we are clearly able to get through this from all angles and in the process will continue to learn. No affliction shall stop me or anyone from carrying forward.

March 24, 2005

With each day I have found my physical condition deteriorating. From my waist down is gone. **I met with the surgeon "Dr. M" this week and scheduled surgery for next Tuesday.** It's a blessing in that I cannot wait much longer. This past weekend I fell in the bathroom hitting my head and breaking it open. Each step is dangerous. My knees lock to stop me from falling as I take each step gingerly. I cannot get up and down stairs and the thought of doing so scares the hell out of me for fear of tumbling down helplessly. To get down I must sit and pull each leg and feet to the next step as I slide down assisted by my arms. Going upstairs at the end of each night, Monica stays behind me as I go up like a Seal, pulling my body up each step, as my lower half drags along. At the top of the stairs I rested, catching my breath. I then crawled and [waived] to Gregory outside his room. I then pulled myself into Alyssa's room using the hamper to brace my body and blow her a kiss. I then crawled into our room and fell on the floor to rest with Monica at my side.

Emotionally, today was rough. I spent the day at the office attempting to wrap things up and I spent most of the day doing what I do best … helping others. Despite my personal problems, I helped others with [theres] taking call after call from clients who needed instant help by way of my advice. Despite my own afflictions, I put that aside so as to extend as much passion and commitment to them to help them through their problems. I love people and strive to help them.

With surgery less than 4 days away, I am prepared mentally to go forward. I trust and pray that God will watch over me as well as all my relatives and friends in heaven. Regardless of the outcome, I am truly blessed for what I have, and have been given. LIFE IS GREAT!!

March 28, 2005 *"Surgery Number 1"*

The first surgery on a Monday was an angiogram where they went through the groin muscle to see if they can shut off the blood supply to the tumors before surgery to minimize the chance of bleeding. They determined it was unnecessary to do the second step "embolism" (Cutting off the blood supply).

March 29, 2005 *"Surgery Number 2"*

10 Hour surgery performed today on my spine by Dr. M to remove the tumor from my spinal cord. My faith is in the Lord and my body is in the hands of the Doctor. It was a 10 hour surgery where Dr. M removed tennis ball size tumor from my spine which was impinging on the spinal cord causing various degrees of paralysis to various parts of my body. Despite this, my will power, determination was at an all time high.

April 18, 2005 *"Where do I begin"*

As I sit here in the hospital writing this it is almost a month after the last entry, 3 surgeries later.

June 3, 2005

I am now home. It is difficult to put into concise words the last 2 months, but I will try. The major surgery was on March 29, 2005 It was a 10 hour surgery where Dr. M removed a tennis ball size tumor from my spine which was impinging on the spinal cord which was the reason I was unable to walk. The surgery was nothing short of a miracle. He went in from the back (8–10 inch scar), then from the side. He removed 1 rib in the process. He took a piece of my hip and fused it with a piece of a cadaver to my spine. He then held it in place with a titanium rod and screws. In the end, I had a scar on my back, on my ribs and on my lower left side. Unfortunately, I developed an infection within the wound site. A staff] infection of this sort can cause all sorts of problems including additional paralysis, or death. As a result, they had to perform surgery number 3 where they went in, cleaned out the site to get out the infection as well as placing me on some heavy duty antibiotics. While in the hospital, I finally went from floor 7 (absolutely terrible) to the 5th floor, the rehabilitation unit. Here it was great and made up of incredibly dedicated and caring people, unlike floor 7 which consisted of rude, unprofessional and overworked people who clearly gave off an attitude and dislike of their jobs. On the 5th floor I began physical therapy (with Boris, a huge, really cool guy) and occupational therapy (with Colleen), whereby both were incredibly kind, compassionate and dedicated to their work. I again contracted another infection.

As I sit here today, almost 2 months after surgery, the wound is still not closed and I am still getting fevers. Time will tell whether I need surgery number 4 to remove the titanium rod which they believe is the current source of the infection. In essence, I had to retrain my entire body to work again. To lift something up, to walk, to stand up, to eat, get dressed and perform the most basic things takes a long time. We take things for granted in life. When you're thirsty, you simply get up, reach for a glass and pour some water and drink. Now, this process takes about 20 minutes. I work day in and day out in therapy and have been outperforming their expectations. "Try to do 3 reps … I do 10", "try to walk 5 feet with assistance on the side bars, I walked 20 feet without assistance". The years of conditioning my body, and the much touted "muscle memory" was true. My body was now regenerating itself with the assistance of the parts that were not affected. Therapy was long, hard, painful and intense, but I loved every second of it. I eventually migrated to what I do best, helping others. I befriended several older patients and assisted them, encouraged them and gave them hope. I became the leader in the classes and assisted the therapists in motivating the others. I wheeled myself from room to room trying to find something positive or encouraging to say to my fellow patients.

Here's where it gets good! Sleep deprivation, spiders and paranoia!

After the big surgery, I was sent to the ICU unit. With anesthesia they place a large metal tube down your throat to assist you to breathe during the surgery. When I woke, my throat felt like I could not breathe or swallow. I constantly had to drink water to open my airway. I was panicking that if I did not have my water, I would not live, as I believed I could not breathe. As an aside, my entire life, I have always been totally independent and the one who always made the decisions for everyone else. I was now the complete opposite, unable to move and under the total control of the hospital staff and Doctors. While Monica, or my Dad was there, I was fine, because they would assure I had water. The hospital would not let them stay however after a certain hour at night. I need to insure that you understand just how intense a fear I had. I was convinced, without periodic sips of water, I was going to die! I have never before had such an intense fear. Additionally, it was not like I could simply reach for some water and drink. Just coming out of a major surgery where my body was torn, twisted, things removed and the like for 10 hours, I was unable to move my arms, or anything, in my right hand I had a button to push which would inject Morphine directly into my bloodstream. Whenever I could push it, I did as I was in a state of immense pain and confusion coming out of the anesthesia.

As I continue with the events of the day, I want to make sure you understand that writing this now, well after the fact, it is almost surreal that this was occurring. Although I was assured later that I was breathing fine, and was being closely monitored, at that time, I was absolutely convinced otherwise. Before Monica and Dad left, they set me up with big glasses of water plus bottled water. As they left, the fear in my mind was at an all time high. At that time, I convinced myself that it was me against the hospital. I would not let myself go to sleep under any circumstances for fear of death should I do so. Despite being in ICU, the care was terrible. Night 1 was fine as Monica was allowed to stay and the nurse was great. In ICU, I was hooked up to several monitors with various things being injected in various IV's. When a monitor would sense a problem, it would beep loudly, simultaneously sending a signal to the nurse's desk whereby they would (or should) come in immediately. On night 1, each time the monitor went off, the angelic nurse was immediately there to address the problem thereby giving me a sense of confidence. Night 2 was radically different. The machines would beep and the nurse would NOT come in right away, and sometimes not at all. Unlike night 1 where the nurse allowed Monica to stay, on night 2, they would not allow it. At this point, I had not slept for over 18 hours. I could hear the nurses all sitting around outside talking and laughing but NOT coming in when the machine beeped. I still would not allow myself to sleep under any circumstances. Although they pleaded with me to rest and go to sleep, I would not. I kept all of the lights on and the TV to help keep me awake.

Midway through the Second night, I asked the nurses to call the emergency room as my needs were not being attended to. At this point, sleep deprivation was beginning to cause me to be incredibly paranoid and irrational. Reality was slipping away and my mind was converting into a world filled with fright, delusion and severe paranoia. I was told later that all of this was a normal byproduct of the surgeries I had and symptomatic of classic sleep deprivation. When the mind and body is deprived of rest, normalcy erodes and taking its place are various symptoms such that I was experiencing. They would not call the ER. Then, almost like a miracle, the kind nurse from night one (who was working in another area of the hospital) made a point to come see me to see how I was doing. I told her what was happening. After she said that she was not allowed to give me a phone, I told her to look at the picture of Alyssa and Gregory that was hanging on my wall and **told her that if I could not get help, they would not have a father!** This kind, compassionate, wonderful human being began to cry and brought me a phone knowing that she could lose her job for doing so. I dialed 911 and told them that I needed help. They declined indicating that I was in the best possible place (ICU) to address my problems. As an aside, I could only imagine what they must have been thinking receiving this type of crazy call. About 3 am I next called Monica. I told her to call 911 and get to the hospital ASAP! The one Doctor who was on call responded and was extremely rude. My stomach was blown up like a balloon with either surgical gasses or otherwise. The doctor, with an attitude said the only thing they could do is to shove a tube down my nose to relieve the pressure in my stomach which would be very painful. I declined.

Monica arrived shortly thereafter and stayed with me till morning. Dad came later that morning and stood vigil with Monica by my side. At this point I was getting significantly worse, slowly slipping into another person living in a world of delusion. It was now more than 24 hours without sleep. I started to see large bugs crawling on the walls as well as other things that were not there. I could see large spiders crawling on the TV, hundreds of them. I knew they were not real (as I told Monica and my Dad) but I saw them nonetheless. I would tell Monica what I was seeing. Everyone was pleading with me to sleep. They slowly increased things in my IV to try to get me to fall asleep however I fought it with every ounce of my energy. As I did, my mind kept slipping further into disarray placing me in a fictitious world that was creating powerful images and plots.

Finally, later in the morning, Dr. M came in to see me. He agreed to allow Monica to stay with me. The nurse now explained why they wanted to use the tube to relieve the pressure in my stomach. They then placed a long tube up my nose and down my throat. Perhaps one of the most irritable and uncomfortable things I have ever endured. For 4 hours, this pumped surgical gasses out of my stomach. The discomfort and pain was unbearable. All at once, I ripped the tube out of my throat. 28 hours without sleep has now pushed me over the edge. I could only imagine the fear and pain that Monica was going through as she stood there seeing nurses and Doctors rushing in from all angles. She sobbed uncontrollably.

Here is where it gets really good. The plot thickens! After ripping the tube out of my nose, they told Monica and my Dad to go outside as they cleaned me up and tried to get me under control.

At this point, my mind had created a delusional belief that all of the hospital staff was trying to kill me. At that time, I truly believed it. Once Monica and my Dad left, the nurse came in and although I'm sure she was doing a great job of attending to my needs, I perceived her pointing to the picture of Alyssa and Gregory saying "Look at them, it will be the last time you will ever see them". I also believed they were saying that they would kill me and make it look like an accident. I believed that the way they were going to kill me was to spray cloraseptic down my throat which would somehow cut off my air supply causing my death. Believing in my head this plot was about to take place I believed I had to leave a clue to Monica and my Dad what they were doing. I then started pulling all 3 IV's out of my arm causing blood to be everywhere creating what must have looked like a homicide scene. People came from all angles. They strapped down both of my wrists although I fought vigorously with them, thrashing, kicking and yelling.

When Monica and my Dad came back, I told them what I believed was happening and [there] plot to kill me. I begged them to release the restraints. They gave Monica the cloraseptic and told her to give it to me. I could only think that they would be successful in giving Monica the thing that would kill me without her even knowing it. Everyone was doing anything to get me to relax and go to sleep. I kept fighting it. Monica thought that by putting my Ipod on and placing the earphones on, it would calm me down. Just then, the nurse that I believed was trying to kill me came in. Believing that she was getting her way and would be successfully killing me, I looked at her (with a gaze that my Dad later described looked like the devil) and cursed at her. Monica chose one of my favorite author's, Robert Kiyosaki and played one of his financial audio books through the earphones from my ipod. They now gave me mega doses of sedatives. I finally drifted off to sleep waking up *periodically hearing Robert Kiyosaki and not being able to move my arms which were still restrained. Somewhat comically now, I believed that this was the afterlife and I would be listening to Robert Kiyosaki for the rest of my life and not be able to move my arms.*

Eventually I would awake in a room where I saw my Dad on a chair and Monica sleeping on another reclining chair. I thought it was dream. Eventually I fully awoke with Monica by my side and with the restraints still on my arms. It was 2 days later in real time. I asked Monica why I was restrained having no recollection about what had happened over the last few days. She got the Nurse who took the restraints off and gave me a sponge bath. Over the next few days I started to ask Monica questions about what I thought was a dream. Obviously it was not as I discovered. I was told that it was severe sleep deprivation which caused the delusions I experienced. It was apparently common. Looking back, I am extremely grateful to all those wonderful nurses who acted nothing but professional in light of my academy award winning performance. Recalling and writing the above makes me think just how powerful the mind is. It can be programmed to create incredible success and likewise can be programmed to destroy. Herein lies the reason why so many criminals, sociopaths and would be criminals appear not to be remorseful. In their minds, they truly believe that what they are doing is ok.

Fast forward to today, my wound is still open but getting better. I am still getting fevers. If this does not get better, they will have to go back in again (surgery number 4) and remove the titanium rods. This foreign object is what causes the infection. The Doctor wants as much time as possible to pass to allow the fusion to adhere before removing the rods.

Physically, I continue to make progress and I get stronger each day. I get winded real easily however as my blood count and endurance is still low. All in all, I AM BLESSED TO BE ALIVE. Monica, my Dad and entire family have been great.

<u>December 28, 2005</u>

… Fast forward 6 months later. I am writing this from our balcony on the "Grandeur of the Seas". With my feet against the glass. I am overlooking the most beautiful, pristine blue water as we head into Casa Maya Mexico. We surprised the kids (Alyssa 8, Gregory 5) for Xmas with a week cruise as we left 5:00 am 12/26/05.

What a difference a year makes. Last Xmas my legs were bad and my body was failing. Today, 4 surgeries later I can walk and function. I am about 70%. I have constant neuropathy (pins and needles and numbness in both legs and feet) and will likely have this for the rest of my life. My spine is in considerable pain daily both at the surgical site and when they took the bone out from my lower back to fuse into my spine. Likewise my side hurts where they removed the rib. Many internal systems remain partially paralyzed. The best medicine remains my mind and my ability to focus on the positive. LIFE IS GREAT.

This view is amazing. I have a 180 degree view of the water with the sun overhead shining everywhere (85 degrees). The sounds of the water below is like a symphony.

It is awesome just spending time together as a family, uninterrupted. In fact, my Blackberry does not receive any signal. Today, we will arrive at Casa Maya and will spend the day on the beach.

As I look over the balcony and see the boat cascade through the ocean leaving its large wake and waves, I can't help but think how life is similar. We each go through our day leaving our own waves. Most things we do will not leave lasting memories, and like the waves created, will eventually return to its original state. However there are those waves that are seen that leave life long memories and moments. As such, in life it is important to insure our waves/wakes make lasting impressions on the world.

December 30, 2005

I write today from our deck by the pool of the "Grandeur of the Seas" on the last day of our cruise. "Life is great" has been a theme this year. It seems strange to be saying this based on the year but it is true. God does not reward us in all areas of our life at once. At any given time we are experiencing good times and not so good times. As I close this entry, I can only say, Thank you God!

Well, there you have it—a single year of my life as captured in the pages of my personal journal. I truly hope that it has helped you see how a journal can be used to memorialize forever life's many adventures and lessons.

Stage I:
The Breakdown Phase

A Letter to Your Soul
Find a quiet place where you can be totally uninterrupted.

    Relax …

        … focus …

            … and get ready to partake in a …

                conversation with your soul.

As we descend through the Breakdown Phase, you will begin to tap emotions you never knew you had. Being Brutally Honest, you *must* first be honest with yourself. Do not hold back. Don't make up a nice story because you think someone else might read it. Through this process, you should begin to shed life's stereotypes. What society (*society* being any outside influences) thinks, should be temporarily shed. You may form the ultimate conclusion that some things society suggests are actually valid and good for you. The difference now, however, is that *you* will make that decision. Today you are being given the power to decide. To be *truly* empowered is euphoric. While in this state, cherish it, embrace it, and utilize it to its fullest capacity. Your goal throughout this entire process is full immersion. You will find throughout this process that your subconscious will attempt to stop you at times from fully participating and opening up in order to save you from reliving painful experiences. You must tell your subconscious that in this environment—the controlled and positive Brutally Honest environment—it is okay to allow this full participation, this full immersion, as it is a necessary part of transcending the self-imposed barriers that have held you back. This will be a journey to find yourself; so have fun, allow your mind to flow freely, and be playful. At other times, let your emotions flow—whether they bring

> *The soul, of origin divine, glorious image, freed from clay, in life's eternal sphere shall shine, a star of day! The sun is but a spark of fire, a transient meteor in the sky; the soul, as its sire, shall never die.*
> —Robert Montgomery

tears or laughter. If you hold back at all, you will be cheating yourself. Remember that no one else will be grading you, and you will determine your ultimate grade.

The desired destination in the Breakdown Phase is your Soul's Core. We have only just begun this inward journey. It's time to tap into the depths of your inner core that you have never gone to before. You must strive with every ounce of your being to break through self-imposed barriers. As a society we have been conditioned to believe, among other things, that men should not cry, women are weaker than men, and we must be serious at all times. As we take this journey, it will be rough at times. Let your guard down; then stretch it down even further. This is where true empowerment will be achieved. You see, true empowerment is euphoric.

Very few of us have ever really connected with our souls. Even fewer have found our Soul's Core. Where is the Core? Is it different for each of us? You bet it is. We are all different. It is for this reason that if we yield to what society says we should do or be, we risk following a course that does not align with our true destiny.

It's time to formally introduce the two of you. In the following letter, fill in the blanks. Even though some things may not totally apply to you, let your mind expand and fill in the missing parts.

Date: _____, 20__
Dear Soul:

It has been a long time since we have spoken. In fact, this is the first time we have consciously spoken. I apologize for the delay. I have been very busy doing all of the things society told me I ought to do to be happy and productive. I have gone to work each day to make enough money to pay the bills each month. If I am lucky, I will have slightly more than I need to put aside for a rainy day. I have been working for money. I have had a life full of ups and downs, happiness and sorrow.

I am writing to you in hopes of getting to know you better. I am sure I will stumble during this process, much the same way I have done in life. Please give me the strength and power to open up through this journey and be Brutally Honest with you. My purpose is to learn more about myself so that I can be a better_____
(example: person, parent, child, friend, lover).

> *Pleasure is very seldom found where it is sought. Our brightest blazes of gladness are commonly kindled by unexpected sparks.*
> —Samuel Johnson

The Past

Greg

I sat in a darkened, quiet, isolated office at Children's Hospital of Philadelphia along with my parents. I was fourteen years old, a freshman in high school, going through all of the typical adjustments that freshmen go through. To me this was just another doctor's appointment, which provided me with a day off from school. A somewhat naïve kid, I was oblivious as to just how significant this day was then and would be for the rest of my life. I sat and read as we waited for the doctor. Leading up to this day were a barrage of tests: MRIs, CT scans, X-rays, bone scans, and a mylegram. My parents, who otherwise were stalwarts of strength and courage, seemed different that day—very different!

When the doctor walked in, you could have heard a pin drop in the quiet office. As he sat down behind his desk, he spoke quietly to my parents out of earshot from me. Just then, my mom broke down in tears with my father holding her, comforting her as tears shed from his own eyes. All I could feel was a sense of embarrassment as I sat there dumbfounded as to what had occurred. My mom got out of her seat, came up to me, and embraced me for what felt like hours and just continued to cry. My dad followed suit. As both of them thanked the doctor profusely, we left.

It wasn't until many months—perhaps years—later that I understood exactly what it was the doctor had told my parents. I had gone to the doctor weeks earlier with a painful condition known as shingles, and it was discovered that there were various tumors in my lower spine and ribs. They had thought it was cancer and had braced my parents for the worst, setting up all the tests leading to this fateful visit with the doctor. The news that the doctor gave my parents that day, after all that worry and anticipation was that it was *not* cancer! Being a parent now, I can only imagine the immense pain my parents must have gone through as they counted the hours until the results would be revealed.

The doctors did discover, however, that I had a rare condition. I was—and still remain—the only person in the world with this incredibly painful and debilitating condition, which necessitates radiation therapy, experimental treatments, and countless tests and follow-ups and causes periods of disability.

This however was my defining moment—a moment that has positively affected every facet of my life. What defining moments in your life have shaped who you are today?

Brutally Honest Life Management Journal

Soul, I need your help in sorting out my past. When I think back, my earliest memories are:

_____
_____
_____
_____
_____
_____

Think about your earliest memories, maybe in your first home with your parents and siblings, in a schoolyard, in a hospital, or any number of places. In the space above, immediately write in detail the first vision that comes to mind. (Don't spend too much time on this.)

What did you write? Were they happy memories or sad? Did they include others? Who? Are you inside or outside in these memories? Is your vision bright and vivid, or is it black and white? Is it something you're proud of or ashamed of? Remember, this is your personal journal, no one else's. Don't hold back. For perhaps the first time in your life, I want you to be Brutally Honest.

Wow. I haven't thought about these things in a long time. When I think about these first memories, I become very _____. This process has gotten me thinking. My past was filled with many emotions. While I may not be the best at communicating these things, I want to share with you some of my memories of my past.

My father's name was/is: _____.

He was born on _____ (date) in _____ (place).

My father's occupation(s) was/were: _____.

My childhood memories about my father are:

_____
_____
_____
_____

A typical day for my father was:

_____
_____
_____
_____

The things I learned from my father are/were:

_____
_____
_____

Because of my father, today I am:

_____
_____
_____

I always think of my father whenever:

_____
_____
_____

My mother's name was/is: _____.
She was born on _____(date) in _____(place).
My mother's occupation(s) was/were: _____
_____.

My childhood memories about my mother are:

_____
_____
_____

A typical day for my mother was:

_____
_____
_____

The things I learned from my mother are/were:

_____
_____
_____

Because of my mother, today I am:

_____

I always think of my mother whenever:

I have _____ siblings.

Their names are:

My childhood memories of my siblings are:

Growing up, my favorite family tradition was:

My memories of my childhood home(s) are:

I loved when our family went to _____ _____, because: _____

My friends growing up were:
_____
_____

The things we did were:
_____
_____

Spiritually, my beliefs growing up were:
_____
_____

I went to the following schools:
_____
_____

When I think of my school(s), I:
_____
_____

The first occupation I can recall wanting to be was:
_____
_____

I wanted to be this occupation because:
_____
_____

My first job was: _____.
Growing up, I was taught the following about money:
_____
_____

Brutally Honest Life Management Journal

> *However learned or eloquent, man knows nothing truly that he has not learned from experience.*
> —Christopher Martin Wieland

The Painful Past

> ### *Jim*
>
> I can remember the touch of her hand and the warm feeling I had when I came through the door from school and she was there to meet me. She made my life good, and she made me feel that I was special—and to her, I was.
>
> My mother, Donna Grim, was the type of mother that every child longs to have. She was extremely loving, but she knew where to draw boundaries and be a parent. You could say that she spoiled me with constant attention, and you would be right. However she also taught me discipline and the difference between right and wrong.
>
> As I tried to run from my past I could never run from her. When she left this world to be with God, a part of me left as well. This part of my past was gone forever. Even though she was gone, her presence was with me daily, and this part of my past helps to shape the person I am and what I do. Sometimes we try to run from our past and end up running in circles.
>
> Take some time to really feel and embrace your past as you work through the next exercise.

Unfortunately, Soul, there have been some sad and/or upsetting memories of things that caused me pain (emotional and/or physical). I think my mind repressed a lot of them because it took some deep thought to evoke them. Likewise, it took great strength and courage for me to put these in writing, especially the things I am ashamed of.

My most painful memories of my past (or things that I may not be proud of) are:

1) _____
2) _____
3) _____
4) _____
5) _____

Next to each one above, I placed a number between one and one hundred—one for the most innocent thing causing very little, if any, pain and one hundred indicating the most painful experience that one can imagine.

While these memories are all significant, I must say that the following three memories caused me the most pain (emotional, physical, or both), with the first being the most painful:

1) _____
2) _____
3) _____

I chose these three because:

_____
_____
_____
_____
_____

Now that I see these three in writing, in front of me, I can see that they all share the following traits (feelings of loneliness, being overwhelmed, depression, anger, discomfort, fear, hurt, frustration, disappointment, lack of fulfillment, lack of excitement, loss, guilt, regret, or inadequacy, for example):

_____
_____
_____

Out of the traits they share, the following seems to be the one that appears in each and is the central cause of the painful memories: _____.

I could definitely see a change in my physiology and my state of mind when I was thinking about these things and writing them.

My body language included: (Slumped shoulders? A frown? Arms tightly folded?)

_____
_____
_____

My breathing was: (Shallow? Slow? Fast?)

_____
_____
_____

Despite the consequences of the above traits, and subsequent emotions, I feel better having gone through them because:

_____
_____

Although I know I was ultimately responsible for my emotions and how I dealt with each situation, I also had help from the following people (include each person's name and relationship to you):

It was important to have the help of these individuals because:

In addition to these individuals, I utilized the support of (books, audio programs, or seminars, for example):

> *Experience is not what happens to you; it is what you do with what happens to you.*
> —Aldous Huxley

The Pleasant Past

Jim

The doctor looked at me and said, "It's time, Jim. Let's go." I wanted to run. I wanted to say no, but of course I followed him into the room where my first daughter, Meghan, would come into this world. My former wife and the mother of my children lay there with a certain calm coolness that made me a bit ashamed of my fear. My fear came from the unknown that accompanies the birth of any child; but here lay this woman, soon to be a mother, and none of that fear was with her. I truly thought that to be amazing, and it further solidified my theory that God grants superpowers to mothers.

Needless to say, Meghan came into this world on April 9, healthy and screaming her little lungs out, and I knew that my life would never be the same. I looked into her little reddened face and saw everything in life that I had ever wanted. To say I was happy would have been an understatement. This day in my past marked a transformation of Jim Grim. This day was not about stock options or huge executive bonuses, but this day was more significant than any other to date. This day was about life in its purest form.

Take this time to look at your pleasant past and enjoy how good life has been to you.

Thankfully, my past was not all painful. To the contrary, my past was also filled with many pleasurable experiences.

My happiest memories of my past are:

1) _____
2) _____
3) _____
4) _____
5) _____

Next to each one above I placed a number between one (indicating the most basic thing causing very little, if any, pleasure) and one hundred (indicating the most pleasurable experience that one can imagine—pure ecstasy).

I'm not sure why I put the pleasurable memories in the order that I did. Was I simply brainstorming, or were they ranked in order of importance? It felt great nonetheless to relive these amazing times from my past. While all five are great memories, I must say that the following three are my favorites, with the first being my all-time favorite:

1)_____
2)_____
3)_____

Now that I have recalled these amazing moments, I will close my eyes and fully engage all of my senses to firmly entrench in my deepest subconscious just how pleasant and powerful these memories are; thus, I may recall these memories at any time in the future.

I chose these three because:
_____
_____
_____

Now that I see these three in writing, in front of me, I can see that they all share the following pleasurable traits:
_____
_____
_____

Out of the traits that they share, the following is my favorite:
_____
_____
_____

I chose this as my favorite because: _____
_____
_____.

Much the same way that the painful memories adversely affected me, I could definitely see positive changes in my physiology when I was thinking and writing about these pleasurable things.

My body language was as follows: (Sat erect? Relaxed arms? Smiled?)
_____
_____
_____

My breathing was: (Slow? Relaxed?)
_____

Brutally Honest Life Management Journal

_____
_____

Like my recall of the painful memories, I again recognize and take responsibility for my emotions and how I dealt with each situation. In forming these lasting, pleasurable memories, I also had help from the following people (include each person's name and relationship to you):
_____
_____
_____

These individuals were important in forming these lasting memories because:
_____
_____
_____

In addition to these people, I utilized the support of (books, audio programs, or seminars, for example):
_____
_____
_____

When I sat back and looked at all ten memories, painful and pleasurable, I realized that they all combined to form my personality. How I react to situations,

> *Learn from yesterday, live for today, hope for tomorrow. The important thing is not to stop questioning.*
> —Albert Einstein

interact with others, and conduct myself and all aspects of my being were shaped by my past. (Rewrite the three most painful and most pleasurable memories below.)

Painful memories:
1)_____
2)_____
3)_____

Pleasurable memories:
1)_____
2)_____
3)_____

If I honestly rank the six combined from one (the most influential moment that has shaped my personality) to six (the least influential episode that has shaped my personality), I would list them as follows, placing a "PA" next to all painful memories and a "PL" next to all pleasurable ones:

1) _____
2) _____
3) _____
4) _____
5) _____
6) _____

I ranked them this way because:

_____
_____
_____

I can see now how differently my life might be today if the priority given to each memory above shifted. By switching number six with number one, how would that have changed things? Would this be better or worse?

_____
_____
_____

Rewrite the six, listing the top three pleasurable traits in the first three positions followed by the top three painful traits.

1) _____
2) _____
3) _____
4) _____
5) _____
6) _____

If my past reflected the above, as opposed to my initial rankings, my life would be different in the following ways:

_____
_____
_____
_____
_____
_____
_____

Brutally Honest Life Management Journal

If I had a magic button that would allow me to rewrite my past, I would change the following:

_____
_____
_____
_____
_____
_____

    Soul, I hope you can see that I am trying my best to get to the core of you. It's much tougher than I thought. I must say, however, that the simple act of writing my thoughts down in this letter to you has been a catharsis of sorts. I didn't realize just how emotionally charged my past was.

    I know now that my present is the sum total of my past and personal and societal conditioning, whether good or bad.

> *A man's genius is always, in the beginning of life, as much unknown to himself as to others; and it is only after frequent trials, attended with success, that he dare think himself equal to those undertakings in which those who have succeeded have fixed the admiration of mankind.*
> —David Hume

Brutally Honest Inventory

> ### *Jim*
>
> I walked into Gregory LaMonaca's law office to meet the man whom my friend said would guide me through the maze of difficulties that custody and divorce hearings would become. I did not know what to expect, but I figured I could handle everything because I am Jim Grim—warrior of the corporate world and eliminator of all that stands in my way. When I left Greg's office I realized that I had much to learn.
>
> Greg LaMonaca is not your typical attorney, if there is such a thing in the world. Greg introduced me to a concept he developed called Brutally Honest, and it positively changed my life forever. Through his initial interview of me as a potential client he made me realize that learning and growing was for everyone and that, if you think you have it made, you might just have *been* made. (Think about that.)
>
> I remember Greg asking me if I ever read motivational books or read books about great leaders. I remember thinking, "Why would I do that when I have me to listen to? I am a great leader, and I trust only me."
>
> When I think back on this statement I am overwhelmed by my stupidity and arrogance. The reality is that many of us live in a world where we start to believe our own self-talk. We stop looking for ways to learn or better ourselves through the thoughts of others. If you want to give yourself a gift that will pay immediate and never-ending dividends, commit to reading a motivational book or listening to a motivational audio book or attending a seminar. You will never regret this decision. Take stock of your Brutally Honest Inventory today and add to it immediately.

Over the years, you may have read many different self-help books, attended seminars, or bought products advertised in infomercials that have influenced who you are today in the present and that were meant to help you deal with physical or emotional issues, weight loss, depression, financial difficulty, or any number of issues. List the most influential of these tools below.

Books:

_____

_____

Brutally Honest Life Management Journal

_____
_____
_____
_____
_____

Audio books or recordings:

_____
_____
_____
_____
_____
_____
_____

Videos or DVDs:

_____
_____
_____
_____
_____
_____
_____

Seminars:

_____
_____
_____
_____
_____
_____

After reviewing your lists above, go back and rank them from most favorite and influential (1) to least favorite and influential (10), writing the number to the right of each.

> *The love of study, a passion which derives fresh vigor from employment, supplies each day and hour with a perpetual source of independent and rational pleasure.*
>
> —Edward Gibson

Soul, I have given a lot of thought to how these things have affected my life, both good and bad. I must say that I did get a lot out of the simple acts of reading, watching, or attending some of them. You have allowed me to realize that I attain what I focus on. (This is the Law of Attraction, a powerful and simple law that has been followed from the earliest of times by the most influential individuals. When I was participating in these things, I was focused on positive things for the most part.) As a result, my endorphins were high, and I felt good about myself. Likewise, at the seminars, while surrounded with other people whom I could relate to, have fun with, and support, I likewise was in an exceptionally high state.

Out of all of the things that I listed above, my favorite five things are the following:

- _____
- _____
- _____
- _____
- _____

Soul, when I ranked these from one (most influential) to five (least influential), I started to realize my best learning style. Some individuals are visual learners and tend to learn and recall things better when they see something (pictures, for example), while others are experiential learners (attending and participating in seminars works well for them). You have helped me determine that I am a _____ learner.

Examples:
- Visual (sight)
- Auditory (hearing)
- Kinesthetic (touch)
- Olfactory (smell)
- Gustatory (taste)

Brutally Honest Life Management Journal

    When I took each of my five favorites and wrote a paragraph about what I liked most about them and why, here is what I found:

1. (Rewrite from above.)
_____
_____
_____
_____
_____
_____

2. (Rewrite from above.)
_____
_____
_____
_____
_____
_____

3. (Rewrite from above.)
_____
_____
_____
_____
_____
_____

4. (Rewrite from above.)
_____
_____
_____
_____
_____
_____

5. (Rewrite from above.)
_____
_____
_____
_____

> *The man who has acquired the habit of study, though for only one hour every day in the year, and keeps to the one thing studied till it is mastered, will be startled to see the progress he has made at the end of a twelvemonth.*
> —Edward George Bulwer-Lytton

The Difference: Brutally Honest versus the Gurus

Greg

Jim and I come from two radically different backgrounds, which although different, have provided us with the tools necessary to positively combat life's many challenges. Brutally Honest was created to fight the onslaught of societal pressures on all of us to be, act, and live as others want us to rather than according to our own standards and beliefs. This attitude was shaped early on by my parents who taught me and my brothers to be true to ourselves, never let obstacles stand in our way, and have a strong faith in God. They taught us that family was not optional and instead formed the place where unconditional love would always reign free. We were taught that when life threw us curveballs and when we messed up, made mistakes, or even got in trouble, they would always stand by our sides—and they have. This foundation has been carried through within my family today, and Monica and I live by these same rules.

Throughout my unique past, I have been tested—and tested often. I was told too many times to recount that with "my condition" I could not and should not do things. I am not suggesting that you should not listen to your doctors, parents, and others who have your best interest at heart. I am suggesting, however, that in the end, it is you—and you alone—who must make the decisions that ultimately will continue to define who you are. Some will be right and others wrong; some will be consistent with others' advice. Still others will be radically different; take a look at two examples from my own life:

I was told by my doctor's that with my "condition" I absolutely should not lift weights. Mom totally concurred with the doctors, but Dad backed me and gave me my first set of weights, fueling a love of exercise and a passion for lifting weights. Fast forward to twenty-six years later. I was told that lifting weights was one of the best things I had ever done, as it prepared my body to be strong throughout the many injuries, broken bones, operations, and experimental treatments.

I was also advised that I would be utterly insane to participate in martial arts as one kick to one of the tumors could kill me! Mom again totally concurred with the doctors; Dad reluctantly backed me, with certain rules in place to protect

> me. I went on to obtain my black belt and become a karate instructor. Over the
> next twenty-six years, the physical, philosophical, and mental conditioning that
> the martial arts provided proved over and over to be invaluable in assisting me
> through many of life's challenges.
>
> What defines you? What makes you different? Do you always go with the
> flow, or do you make your own waves? What unique blessings and gifts were you
> given that others don't possess and which allow you to change yourself and the
> world positively?

Soul, I think it was important for me to complete these programs because at least in the moment, I felt good about what I was doing. I was not abusing my body, wasting time in front of the TV or at bars. I question, however, whether I was using my time most effectively. Were the things I was doing best for *me*—or someone else?

Many of these books, recordings, and seminars told me to rank certain categories that *they* said should be important to me. While I did so, I felt empty and confused at the end of the exercises. I found myself feeling as though I could not live up to someone else's standards. Unfortunately, when the hype died down, I was left to accomplish *their* programs, principals, and goals on my own. I then began to change various aspects of my life to try to increase my happiness scores in the areas *they* suggested were lacking. I thought about all of the different things that *they* said I could change. *They* suggested:

- I could lose weight so I could be sexy and good-looking like the models on television and billboards.
- I might earn incredible amounts of money and be able to buy my children the hottest toys.
- I could go to the mall and buy myself everything I thought I needed or that creative marketing suggested I must have.
- I could buy magic weight-loss pills or muscle-enhancement drinks that would give me the perfect body.
- I could aimlessly follow financial advice from the various so-called experts whose counsel appeared on television, in newspapers, and on radio.
- I could be like someone else and never get to really know who I am.

But, in the end I would simply be doing whatever *they* said, never getting to know my Soul's Core. While chasing some of these promises was actually fun, I didn't feel fulfilled or better about myself. Don't get me wrong, in some of the areas that they suggested I should make changes, I did in fact improve somewhat. But, through their exercises, I only learned how to be more like the standard of excellence that they taught—rather than my own. In some of the areas that I improved, while I made some gains, I later found myself slipping further back from where I started.

As I delve down toward your deepest core—no, wait, *our* Soul's Core—I am beginning to see the difference. *Everyone else* has been influencing me, good and bad, from birth until the present. Everywhere I go, I am bombarded with millions of signals per second. Do I want to lose thirty pounds? While it may be healthy to do so (if I am overweight), is it really going to fulfill me and help me get closer to *my* goals and visions? Will the time away from my family that would be necessary to pursue more income really be worth it? While there are an infinite number of things I can do to improve my life, there is also a finite amount of time in each day. It is therefore critical that I focus my time and attention on those things that are the most important to me. You have taught me that I must listen to and attain information from those people in my life who are positive influences. Likewise, I learned that I must use discretion in determining what things in my life add to, rather than take away from, my development.

> *All that a man does outwardly is but the expression and completion of his inward thought. To work effectively, he must think clearly; to act nobly, he must think nobly. Intellectual force is a principle element of the soul's life, and should be proposed by every man as the principal end of his being.*
> —William Ellery Channing

Supercharging Your Batteries

Greg

Anyone who knows me or has visited my home knows that I have a voracious passion for reading and studying about successful people. At any given time, I am reading several books in addition to learning from audio programs and other educational items such as DVDs. I have an unquenchable desire to learn, grow, and help others by sharing my findings with them. I have close friends and family who serve as my mentors, and I meet with them often to get advice, share advice, and continue to learn and grow. I also serve as a mentor to many others who want to learn and commit to utilizing the information.

Monica and I work together as a team along with our children to fuel the family unit. We share everything. It's not what is hers and what is mine; it is ours. She is my best friend and has been since I met her at age fourteen. We learn together as husband and wife and, as parents, share our knowledge with our children. Like other families, we go through trials and tribulations, confront scheduling conflicts, lose loved ones, confront illness, and have had many hurdles to overcome. We have made many mistakes, and we have shared many rewarding times. Our family provides a safety net to each of us; we all know that regardless of life's many curve balls, we are always here for each other.

This immersion in a positive environment has helped me stay focused, grounded, and on track. When I encounter obstacles, feel bad, get off track, or am simply having a bad week, day, or month, it is through reimmersion in all of the things mentioned above that I get back on track. I am not suggesting that this approach is the only approach or even the right approach for you. To the contrary, Brutally Honest is founded upon a belief that you must find what is right for you.

Who do you listen to? What information do you study? What are your hobbies and passions? What do you do in your spare time? Who are you spending your time with? The answers to these questions will go a long way toward determining who you are and to what extent you achieve your life's purpose and toward further defining and shaping you.

It gets tough at times determining what influences in my life—both individuals and things—I should listen to or use. As I get closer to you, however, I am getting better at doing this. To help me better understand and evaluate these influences, I have created a vision of the world's most supercharged batteries. These batteries, unlike most, have the power to take me to the highest levels of my destiny. When supercharged, they have the power to accelerate me through any of my self-imposed limitations and barriers and to provide me with unbelievable potential.

On the other hand, when my batteries lose power, I feel sad and depressed—at my lowest and least productive point. However, as I do the things that positively affect me and interact with positive people, my battery levels increase; life abounds with happiness, success, energy, and unlimited potential. There are many things that affect my battery levels. My batteries are never totally depleted; nor are they always supercharged. An individual's levels are constantly changing. I have come to realize that my own levels change almost in a wavelike pattern, constantly ebbing and flowing. I have found as long as I stay in this middle ground, I am my happiest. It is when I drift too far up or down that I have problems. As a result, I strive to stay in this middle ground.

Each day, as I interact with the various people in my life and am inundated with all of life's things, all of our batteries are in constant flux. These things include every stimulus that confronts me each day—television, the Internet, advertisements, cell phones, video games, bad food, alcohol, drugs, problems at work, and every other conceivable thing. I have found that all positive experiences increase my battery levels while the negative experiences deplete them. I am so sorry for putting you through those times. I know that through my actions I am taking away your power; you need the batteries to stay alive. I truly don't want this to happen. I try very hard to keep you energized, but at times, I simply slip up. I thank you from the bottom of my heart for never allowing me to totally deplete you.

> *The greatest events of an age are its best thoughts. Thought finds its way into action.*
> —Boise

The Present:
Brutally Honest Net-Life Statement

Greg

As I lecture daily to family, friends, and clients, your life is the sum total of all of the parts, not just one of them. I call these parts Brutally Honest Target Zones. Imagine a pie that represents your whole life. Each slice represents the various areas of your life: family, finances, career, health, and other factors unique to you. When you are confronted with a perceived or real crisis, you typically zoom in on the one slice of the pie that is currently in crisis. It is easy to see how doing this would lead someone to feel depressed.

In working with these individuals, I get them to zoom out and look at the whole pie. Then I have them focus on what is going right as opposed to what is going wrong. After that, I have them zoom in on a slice that is going exceptionally well. Once there, I engage all their senses, asking them to describe the personal traits that helped them to create these positive results. I explain to them that these traits are like ingredients in a recipe. I tell them of my world-famous "cheesy omelet," which my daughter loves me to make for her. The ingredients consist of two eggs, milk, spray oil, and cheese. These ingredients collectively make up the perfect omelet … or do they? Actually, they only make the perfect omelet if used in the right order and in the right amounts. If I throw the eggs on the ground, spray the oil in the air, and fry the cheese in the pan by itself, I won't produce the ultimate omelet. By using the same ingredients, in the right amounts, in the right way, and in the right order, I perfectly replicate the ultimate omelet each and every time.

Life works much the same way as creating the ultimate omelet. By asking a person to determine what ingredients make up the slice of life that is going very well and in what order to apply what quantities, we identify the makings for the ultimate slice of pie. Once I've gone through this with someone, I have him or her zoom out again from the ultimate slice, look at the whole pie, and then zoom back in on the slice that is causing problems. We then simply apply the same ingredients from the ultimate slice (which, for example, may be courage, character, tenacity, commitment, or loyalty) to the troubled slice, in the same

> order and in the same quantities. This approach has helped countless individuals to begin the process—sometimes instantaneously—of correcting problem areas in their lives.
>
> When confronted with a problem or crisis, do you allow it to overtake your entire life or do you put it in perspective? Do you consciously visualize similar problems you have encountered in the past that you successfully overcame or do you dwell on the new crisis as if it is the end of the world?

Soul, I feel like we are getting closer by the minute. It helped a great deal to analyze my past. I realize that a lot of my existing personality traits were formed many years ago. It wasn't until I saw them in writing that I could see this.

Through the examination of my past, I am better able to analyze where I am presently. I know that in order to figure out where I ultimately want to go, I must be as open and honest with you in assessing my present as I was in examining my past. I will need your continued help in figuring out where I am today. I know it will do no good to say that things are better or worse than they actually are. I must accurately assess where I really am *today*. This honest assessment will form a strong foundation to gauge my progress moving forward.

When I was listening to those financial gurus on television, they said that I should create a net worth statement. They said that this would be helpful in that it would give a realistic overview of my finances. It would help me in determining whether I have more assets than debt (a positive net worth) or more debt than assets (a negative net worth). This struck me as being a valuable exercise. The exercise helped me clearly see for the first time where I was financially, where I was okay, and where I needed improvement.

This got me thinking: if a net worth statement could give me a clear picture of where my finances are currently, then why couldn't I apply this same thinking to my entire life? So, to assist me in my search to reach your Core, my Soul's Core, I have developed my Net Life Statement. I hope you will bear with me again as I try to open up to you so that I can truly give you a Brutally Honest assessment.

Of course, there are different categories of both people and things in my life. As far as people are concerned, while there are many, the major ones are family members, friends, and work associates. By getting to know you better, I am learning to recognize in advance how to identify those people and things in my life that energize our batteries and those that put a drain on them.

The top three individuals from my family who have positively influenced me and

who help to charge my batteries are:
_____
_____
_____

These people have influenced me so positively because:
_____
_____
_____
_____
_____

What I have learned from determining who in my family influences me most is that: _____
_____
_____
_____
_____

Some things I do to keep the batteries charged with these individuals are:
_____
_____
_____
_____
_____
_____

I commit today to do the following things to attempt to supercharge my batteries with these people:
_____
_____
_____
_____
_____
_____

The top three friends who have positively influenced me and helped to charge my batteries are:
_____
_____
_____

These people have influenced me so positively because:
___
___

Determining which of my friends influence me most has shown me:
___
___
___
___
___

Some things I do to keep the batteries charged with these friends are (for example, meeting weekly to catch up, making sure to remember special events in their lives, and always being there for them even during busy times):

> *He who has imagination without learning has wings and no feet.*
> —Joseph Joubert

___
___

To supercharge my batteries (relationships) with these people, I commit today to do the following things (for example, sending them letters outlining the things you admire about them or telling them often how great it is to have them in your life and citing examples)

> *Of course there is no formula for success except, perhaps, an unconditional acceptance of life and what it brings.*
> —Arthur Rubinstein

___
___
___

The top three individuals from my work or school who have positively influenced me and who help to charge my batteries are:
___
___

These people have influenced me so positively because:

_____
_____
_____
_____
_____

What I have learned from determining who at my work or school most influences me is that:

_____
_____
_____
_____
_____

Some things I do to keep the batteries charged with these individuals are:

_____
_____
_____
_____
_____

I commit today to do the following things to supercharge my batteries with these people:

_____
_____
_____
_____
_____

There are also other people who influence me a great deal who are not family members, friends, or co-workers.

The other individuals who have positively influenced me and who help to charge my batteries are:

_____
_____
_____

These people have influenced me so positively because:

What I have learned from determining what other individuals do to influence me is that:

Some things I do to keep the batteries charged with these individuals are:

I commit today to do the following things to attempt to supercharge my batteries with these people:

It's amazing how I am beginning to see what I need to do to keep our batteries charged, Soul, as well as other ways to create new batteries. The exercise above allowed me to see just how fortunate I am to have these people in my life. I have also learned what to do to keep the relationships strong and to continue to evolve.

Things in Life That Charge Our Batteries

> ### *Jim*
>
> The sky was a beautiful blue and the ocean, a surreal green. It was early June; the water temperature was a chilly 64 degrees, so wet suits were in order. My friend and surfing wingman, Stevo, and I were enjoying a nice, clean surf session at Assateague Island (or "Da Teague" as we had nicknamed it years back). The waves were peaking at over three feet and light offshore winds made them seem like liquid glass. Families played on the beach, and the wild Assateague ponies strolled the white sands with not a care in the world. It was one of those days when you just felt good to be alive.
>
> All of the pressures of business, the stock market, family, and friends seemed to just melt away. Surfing charges my batteries and gets me ready to face the next challenge. Do you have something that charges your batteries? Perhaps it is meeting with a friend that does it for you, or maybe it's reading a great book. It really doesn't matter *what* charges your batteries; it does matter that your batteries do get periodically charged.
>
> So many people live their lives draining their batteries and never charging them. So many people live only to make others feel better while they are never fulfilled themselves. My partner and I often see people who have neglected charging their batteries for so long that the charge cells in the batteries can no longer hold a charge. Make sure you take a good look at what charges your batteries and start *today* to give yourself this gift.

Soul, just as I have found that there are family members, friends, and other people who have positively influenced my life, I have also discovered that there are many *things* that have influenced me. As I have gotten to know you better, I have slowly been able to open up to you in a way that I thought I never could. It is difficult to be Brutally Honest at times. I am afraid that I will offend others or appear conceited or self-centered. I have learned that, to the contrary, by opening up to you I am finding my true self. I am likewise gathering increased self-esteem in the process. This self-esteem allows me to focus on my true wishes and desires. I feel free for perhaps the first time of my life. This is my journal, and more important, my life. In this environment, I can speak the truth without repercussions.

I am the only person who will see this, unless I choose otherwise. Therefore, as I am my only judge, I can open up in an unfettered way.

Therefore, should there be a need for money, cars, food, shopping, or other things, I must communicate this to you to continue my learning process. While I realize there are also things that do not contribute positively to my life (which I will address later), for now I will focus on the things that make me feel good.

The things that have positively influenced me the most and that help to charge my batteries are:

_____
_____
_____
_____
_____
_____

These things have influenced me so positively because:

_____
_____
_____

Determining what things influence me has taught me:

_____
_____
_____

These things keep my batteries charged because:

_____
_____
_____

I commit today to do the following things to supercharge my batteries:

_____
_____
_____

The Negative Drain on Our Batteries

Unfortunately, as with some events of the past, there are individuals who create situations that cause us stress or embarrassment and tend to deplete our batteries' resources. In some cases, this depletion may not be extreme, but it is depletion nonetheless. I have been thinking about these individuals as well, and I realize that while I may not be able to eliminate them from my life, once I consciously identify who they are and how they affect me, I can begin to take steps to increase our battery levels in this regard.

I also understand that despite my best efforts, some individuals will not change or want to work with me in charging our batteries. In these cases, I will learn to avoid the things that increase the likelihood of conflict. In the end, I know I will be closer to you, Soul.

I have definitely found that it is much more painful attempting to recall those individuals who deplete our batteries. I also realize, however, that it is critical that I identify these people so that I may begin to stop the acidic erosion of my batteries and move forward to recharge them.

Listing an individual below does not mean that I don't like or love him or her. I am listing certain individuals in order to be Brutally Honest—so that I may attempt to change the things that cause conflict and avoid these triggers in the future. My purpose is to ultimately enhance our relationship with them.

> *We first make our habits, and then our habits make us. All habits gather, by unseen degrees, as brooks make rivers, rivers run into seas.*
> —John Dryden

Family Members Who Drain Our Batteries

Jim

I clearly remember the feeling I would get when my father was going away on business. Frankly, I was elated that he would be gone. When my father was home, our house was a place where you had to be careful to say the right things and make sure you kept your head down. Just the thought of having to go to the store with him—just the two of us—made me feel sick. To this day I can't say that I know what it was that made me feel this way about him, but when I was around him, I could feel my batteries draining at a rapid rate.

My father was an only child, born into a life a luxury. His father, my Grandfather Grim, was a doctor, and he provided a life for my father and grandmother that was quite good. To give you an example, my grandparents were the first on their block to get a color television (or so I'm told). My grandfather was a robust man who went to college early on a scholarship and then graduated near the top of his class at Jefferson Medical School. People in town loved "Old' Doc Grim," and he seemed bigger then life to me. My father, on the other hand, was given everything and tried next to nothing. He never measured up to the expectations my grandfather put on him, and I believe this is where my father learned to be negative.

My father would tell me how he hated his father and how they never did anything together. My father's account of my grandfather was that he was a hard-drinking womanizer who was only concerned about being a doctor. As I sat and listened to this, I would think to myself how ironic the situation was. My father hated his father, and now I hated my father. From a very early age, I vowed that, if I were blessed with children, I would be a good father and help to recharge their batteries.

The top three individuals from my family who have caused a drain on my batteries are:

_____
_____
_____

I realize that to change the patterns that cause me pain, I must begin to understand what triggers were present in the past that caused my batteries to drain with these individuals. Soul, if I can learn what has caused problems in the past, then I will be able to avoid these situations proactively in the future, and to the extent I find myself in conflict with these individuals, I will be better able to diffuse the situation.

To begin to better understand these things, I submit to you the following self-analysis about these three family members:

Name of first family member: _____

Relationship to me: _____

I have known this person for _____ years.

This person is important in my life because:

_____
_____
_____
_____
_____

If this person were no longer in my life, it would impact me in the following ways:

_____
_____
_____
_____
_____

An example of a time when my batteries were drained when interacting with this individual is below.

Date: _____

The situation:

_____
_____
_____
_____
_____

This caused me so much pain because:

_____
_____
_____

Brutally Honest Life Management Journal

_____
_____
_____

I would say that this event, at the time it occurred, caused me pain at this level (on a scale from one, representing absolutely no pain, to one hundred, representing the most horrendous pain imaginable): _____

> To forgive is powerful, liberating, and empowering. If each day you are given a full glass of water, and the water represents all of the energy and effort you may expend in that day, to dwell in the past will surely empty the glass quickly, leaving little for progress. On the contrary, to forgive will keep the glass full and will refill the empty glasses of others, ensuring it will overflow into tomorrow.
> —Gregory LaMonaca

As I am writing this today, I would say that the pain is at this level (using the same scale): _____.

When I look back on this event, I would say I was responsible for _____ percent of the problem while the other person involved was responsible for _____ percent of the problem.

Looking back, I can see that what triggered the event was:
_____
_____
_____
_____

Now that I have taken the time to look carefully at what triggered the event, I can see that if only the following had occurred, we could have avoided the problem altogether:
_____
_____
_____
_____

In the future, I will do the following to keep such an occurrence from happening:
_____

_____
_____
_____

Now that I have analyzed it, I can see that this event was actually not as bad as I thought because:

_____
_____
_____
_____
_____

Now, after carefully analyzing the situation, I would rank the event at this level: _____

Name of second family member: _____

Relationship to me: _____

I have known this person for _____ years.

This person is important in my life because:

_____
_____
_____
_____
_____

If this person were no longer in my life, it would impact me in the following ways:

_____
_____
_____
_____

An example of a time when my batteries were drained when interacting with this individual is below.

Date:_____

The situation:

_____
_____
_____

Brutally Honest Life Management Journal

This caused me so much pain because:
_____
_____
_____
_____

I would say that this event, at the time that it occurred, caused me pain at this level (on a scale from one, representing absolutely no pain, to one hundred, representing the most horrendous pain imaginable): _____

As I am writing this today, I would say that the pain is at this level (on the same scale): _____

When I look back on this event, I would say I was responsible for _____ percent of the problem while the other person involved was responsible for _____ percent of the problem.

Looking back, I can see that what triggered the event was:
_____
_____
_____
_____

Now that I have taken the time to look carefully at what triggered the event, I can see that if only the following had occurred, we could have avoided the problem altogether:
_____
_____
_____
_____

In the future, I will do the following to keep such an occurrence from happening:
_____
_____
_____
_____

Now that I have analyzed it, I can see that this event was actually not as bad as I thought because:
_____
_____

Now, after carefully analyzing the situation, I would rank the event at this level: _____

Name of third family member: _____

Relationship to me: _____

I have known this person for _____ years.

This person is important in my life because:
_____
_____
_____
_____.

If this person were no longer in my life, it would impact me in the following ways:
_____
_____
_____
_____.

An example of a time when my batteries were drained when interacting with this individual is below.

Date: _____

The situation:
_____
_____
_____
_____.

This caused me so much pain because:
_____
_____
_____
_____.

I would say that this event, a the time that it occurred, caused me pain at this level (on a scale from one, representing absolutely no pain, to one hundred, representing the most horrendous pain imaginable: _____.

As I am writing this today, I would say that the pain is at this level (on the same scale): _____.

Brutally Honest Life Management Journal

When I look back on this event, I would say I was responsible for _____ percent of the problem while the other person involved was responsible for _____ percent of the problem.

Looking back, I can see that what triggered the event was:

_____.

Now that I have taken the time to look carefully at what triggered the event, I can see that if only the following had occurred, we could have avoided the problem altogether:

_____.

In the future, I will do the following to keep such an occurrence from happening:

_____.

Now that I have analyzed it, I can see that this event was actually not as bad as I thought because:

_____.

Now, after carefully analyzing the situation, I would rank the event at this level: _____.

> *The family is the association established by nature for the supply of man's everyday wants.*
> —Aristotle

Friends Who Drain Our Batteries

The three friends who have caused the most drain on my batteries are:
_____
_____
_____

Like I did when analyzing my family, I must attempt to determine the triggers that have caused problems in the past with these friends.

To begin to better understand these things, I submit to you the following self-analysis about these three friends:

Name of first friend: _____

Relationship to me: _____

I have known this person for _____ years.

This person is important in my life because:
_____
_____
_____
_____
_____
_____
_____.

If this person were no longer in my life, it would impact me in the following ways:
_____
_____
_____
_____
_____
_____
_____.

An example of a time when my batteries were drained when interacting with this individual is below.

Date_____

The situation:
_____
_____
_____
_____

Brutally Honest Life Management Journal

This caused me so much pain because:

_____
_____
_____
_____

I would say that this event, at the time that it occurred, caused me pain at this level (on a scale from one, representing absolutely no pain, to one hundred, representing the most horrendous pain imaginable): _____.

As I am writing this today, I would say that the pain is at this level (on the same scale): _____.

When I look back on this event, I would say I was responsible for _____ percent of the problem while the other person involved was responsible for _____ percent of the problem.

> *Never explain. Your friends do not need it and your enemies will not believe you anyway.*
> —Elbert Hubbard

Looking back, I can see that what triggered the event was:

_____
_____
_____
_____.

Now that I have taken the time to look carefully at what triggered the event, I can see that if only the following had occurred, we could have avoided the problem altogether:

_____
_____
_____
_____.

In the future, I will do the following to keep such an occurrence from happening:

_____
_____
_____
_____

Now that I have analyzed it, I can see that this event was actually not as bad as I thought because:

_____
_____
_____

Now, after carefully analyzing the situation, I would rank the event at this level: _____.

Name of second friend:_____

Relationship to me:_____

I have known this person for _____ years.

This person is important in my life because:

_____
_____
_____
_____

If this person were no longer in my life, it would impact me in the following ways:

_____
_____
_____
_____

An example of a time when my batteries were drained when interacting with this individual is below.

Date:_____

The situation:

_____
_____
_____
_____

This caused me so much pain because:

_____
_____
_____
_____

I would say that this event, at the time that it occurred, caused me pain at

Brutally Honest Life Management Journal

this level (on a scale from one, representing absolutely no pain, to one hundred, representing the most horrendous pain imaginable): _____

As I am writing this today, I would say that the pain is at this level (on the same scale): _____

When I look back on this event, I would say I was responsible for _____ percent of the problem while the other person involved was responsible for _____ percent of the problem.

Looking back, I can see that what triggered the event was:

_____
_____
_____
_____

Now that I have taken the time to look carefully at what triggered the event, I can see that if only the following had occurred, we could have avoided the problem altogether:

_____
_____
_____
_____

In the future, I will do the following to keep such an occurrence from happening:

_____
_____
_____
_____

Now that I have analyzed it, I can see that this event was actually not as bad as I thought because:

_____
_____
_____
_____

Now, after carefully analyzing the situation, I would rank the event at this level: _____

Name of third friend: _____
Relationship to me: _____
I have known this person for _____ years.

This person is important in my life because:
_____
_____
_____
_____

If this person were no longer in my life, it would impact me in the following ways:
_____
_____
_____
_____

An example of a time when my batteries were drained when interacting with this individual is below.

Date:_____

The situation:
_____
_____
_____
_____

This caused me so much pain because:
_____
_____
_____
_____

> *Life is not so short but that there is always time for courtesy.*
> —Ralph Waldo Emerson

I would say that this event, at the time that it occurred, caused me pain at this level (on a scale from one, representing absolutely no pain, to one hundred, representing the most horrendous pain imaginable): _____

As I am writing this today, I would say that the pain is at this level (on the same scale): _____

When I look back on this event, I would say I was responsible for _____ percent of the problem while the other person involved was responsible for

Brutally Honest Life Management Journal

_____ percent of the problem.

Looking back, I can see that what triggered the event was:

_____
_____
_____

Now that I have taken the time to look carefully at what triggered the event, I can see that if only the following had occurred, we could have avoided the problem altogether:

_____
_____
_____
_____

In the future, I will do the following to keep such an occurrence from happening:

_____
_____
_____
_____

Now that I have analyzed it, I can see that this event was actually not as bad as I thought because:

_____
_____
_____
_____

Now, after carefully analyzing the situation, I would rank the event at this level: _____

> *Saying is one thing, doing another. We must consider the sermon and the preacher distinctly and apart.*
> —Michel E. de Montaigne

Work Associates Who Drain Our Batteries

Jim

"Hey, Grimmy!" came the loud voice of one of the seasoned engineers, Bob, from across the lab. "Are you done messing up that circuit yet? We need to test the real mission equipment." I was a young engineer at General Electric and in the process of creating equipment that would be used to test the hardware and software that made up the product we were making for our customer. You see, the more seasoned engineers designed and implemented what was called mission critical hardware and software, and the newer engineers, fresh out of school, built test equipment. Since I had just graduated, I fell into the latter category, and Bob, being five years out of college, was building the "real equipment." Of course, Bob never let anyone forget that what he was doing was much more important than the work the newer engineers did.

When Bob's personality became even more of a problem I consulted my friend and associate, Diego. Diego had grown up in a rough area of Philadelphia, and to say that he had not had a silver-spoon childhood would be an understatement. What Diego did have was the ability to look past the obvious flaws in people and see their real potential. Diego helped me see that Bob really was not a bad guy and in some ways he and I were more then work associates. We were friends as well. The problem was that you could never get close to Bob. He was the type of person who would meet people and belittle them without even knowing them. He truly caused a drain on my batteries, yet as I said, I actually had some form of a friendship with him. I think I was friends with him because it was easier them being his enemy. When I look back, I realize that I should have told Bob how I felt, but at the time, I did not have the tools to do that. I would urge you to think about how many people like Bob are currently in your life. Let's continue and get the tools necessary to deal with and even appreciate the Bobs in all of our lives. Remember this: when you are sent a challenge, embrace it and give thanks for the opportunity to grow!

The three work associates who have caused the most drain on my batteries are:

Like I did when analyzing my family and friends, I must again determine the triggers that have caused problems in the past. I submit to you the following self-analysis about these three work associates. (Note: The term *associate* can include co-workers, bosses, or anyone who is affiliated with your work in any manner.):

Name of first work associate: _____

Relationship to me: _____

I have known this person for _____ years.

This person is important in my life because:

_____
_____
_____
_____
_____

If this person were no longer in my life, it would impact me in the following ways:

_____
_____
_____
_____
_____

An example of a time when my batteries were drained when interacting with this individual is below.

Date: _____

The situation:

_____
_____
_____
_____

This caused me so much pain because:

_____
_____
_____

I would say that this event, at the time that it occurred, caused me pain at this level (on a scale from one, representing absolutely no pain, to one hundred, representing the most horrendous pain imaginable): _____

As I am writing this today, I would say that the pain is at this level (on the same scale): _____

When I look back on this event, I would say I was responsible for _____ percent of the problem while the other person involved was responsible for _____ percent of the problem.

Looking back, I can see that what triggered the event was:

_____
_____
_____
_____

Now that I have taken the time to look carefully at what triggered the event, I can see that if only the following had occurred, we could have avoided the problem altogether:

_____
_____
_____
_____

In the future, I will do the following to keep such an occurrence from happening:

_____
_____
_____
_____

> *Speak the truth by all means; be bold and fearless in your rebuke of error, and in your keener rebuke of wrong doing; but be human, and loving, and gentle, and brotherly the while.*
> —William Morley Punshon

Now that I have analyzed it, I can see that this event was actually not as bad as I thought because:

_____
_____
_____

Brutally Honest Life Management Journal

Now, after carefully analyzing the situation, I would rank the event at this level: _____.

Name of second work associate: _____

Relationship to me: _____

I have known this person for _____years.

This person is important in my life because:

_____
_____
_____
_____
_____

If this person were no longer in my life, it would impact me in the following ways:

_____
_____
_____
_____
_____

An example of a time when my batteries were drained when interacting with this individual is below.

Date:_____

The situation:

_____
_____
_____
_____
_____

This caused me so much pain because:

_____
_____
_____
_____

I would say that this event, at the time that it occurred, caused me pain at this level (on a scale from one, representing absolutely no pain, to one hundred, representing the most horrendous pain imaginable): _____

As I am writing this today, I would say that the pain is at this level (on the same scale): _____

When I look back on this event, I would say I was responsible for _____ percent of the problem while the other person involved was responsible for _____ percent of the problem.

Looking back, I can see that what triggered the event was:
_____
_____
_____
_____

Now that I have taken the time to look carefully at what triggered the event, I can see that if only the following had occurred, we could have avoided the problem altogether:
_____
_____
_____
_____

In the future, I will do the following to keep such an occurrence from happening:
_____
_____
_____
_____

Now that I have analyzed it, I can see that this event was actually not as bad as I thought because:
_____
_____
_____
_____

Now, after carefully analyzing the situation, I would rank the event at this level: _____

> *It will usually be found that those who sneer habitually at human nature, and affect to despise it, are among its worst and least pleasant samples.*
> —Charles Dickens

Brutally Honest Life Management Journal

Name of third work associate: _____
Relationship to me: _____
I have known this person for _____ years.
This person is important in my life because:
_____
_____
_____
_____

If this person were no longer in my life, it would impact me in the following ways:
_____
_____
_____
_____

An example of a time when my batteries were drained when interacting with this individual is below.
Date: _____
The situation:
_____
_____
_____
_____

This caused me so much pain because:
_____
_____
_____
_____

I would say that this event, at the time that it occurred, caused me pain at this level (on a scale from one, representing absolutely no pain, to one hundred, representing the most horrendous pain imaginable): _____

As I am writing this today, I would say that the pain is at this level (on the same scale): _____

When I look back on this event, I would say I was responsible for _____ percent of the problem while the other person involved was responsible for _____ percent of the problem.

Looking back, I can see that what triggered the event was:

_____
_____
_____

Now that I have taken the time to look carefully at what triggered the event, I can see that if only the following had occurred, we could have avoided the problem altogether:

_____
_____
_____

In the future, I will do the following to keep such an occurrence from happening:

_____
_____
_____

Now that I have analyzed it, I can see that this event was actually not as bad as I thought because:

_____
_____
_____

Now, after carefully analyzing the situation, I would rank the event at this level: _____

> *There may be luck in getting a good job—but there's no luck in keeping it.*
> —J. Ogden Armour

Brutally Honest Life Management Journal

Things in Life That Drain Our Batteries

Soul, as I have continued my journey to your Core, I have learned so much by opening up to you. So far, I have seen how different family members, friends, and others have contributed to my life, both positively and negatively. I also have seen how the many different things in my life have impacted me.

While it was difficult to be Brutally Honest in telling you the things that were important in my life, it has been equally difficult to acknowledge the things in my life that have caused me pain. All I have to do is turn on the television or read the newspaper to see the many vices that are present in society. Drugs, alcohol, infidelity, abuse, depression, neglect, obesity, anger, greed, envy—this list only scratches the surface. Identifying those things in my life that adversely affect me is an absolute must. I have kept a lot in over the years for fear of the ridicule, embarrassment, or immense pain I associate with revealing it.

As you can see, these are not just physical things; they can be intangible as well. I know that unless I can first acknowledge that these things are present, I will never be able to change the negative impact that they are having on my family, my friends, and me. Bear with me as I open up to you and as I continue to learn and move forward.

You were correct when you taught me that opening up to you would be cathartic—an unveiling of sorts. This is a personal freedom that is unparalleled. As I stated earlier, this is *my* journal and, more important, *my* life. In this environment, I can speak the truth without repercussions, as I am the only person who will see this, unless I choose otherwise. As I am my only judge, I can truly open up.

> *Men are not to be judged by their looks, habit, and appearances; but by the character of their lives and conversations, and by their works. 'Tis better that a man's own works than that another man's words should praise him.*
> —Sir Roger L'Estarnge

I realize that depending on what things I identify, it may be in my best interest to share with others. I know that certain vices, including addictions and abuse, will require the help of professionals such as counselors, or therapists. It is *not* a weakness to open up to these individuals; in fact, it is an incredibly courageous act that will lead to me being able to address these impediments, learn from them, grow, and move forward.

At the *present* time, the ten (or as many as I want to list) most influential things that deplete and drain my batteries are:

_____
_____
_____
_____
_____
_____
_____
_____
_____
_____
_____
_____
_____
_____

    Instead of ranking these experiences from one to ten, I rated the pain of each thing as it exists today (on a scale from one, representing absolutely no pain, to one hundred, representing the most horrendous pain imaginable) and wrote each score next to the item on the list above.

    I next took the five things that have caused me the most pain and rewrote them below with their pain scores written next to each in parenthesis. I then wrote a paragraph for each indicating *how* this thing has adversely affected my life and the people in my life. I have tried very hard to be as vivid as possible in describing the agonizing details.

1. _____(Rewrite from above)
_____
_____
_____

2. _____(Rewrite from above)
_____
_____
_____

3. _____(Rewrite from above)
_____
_____
_____

4. _____(Rewrite from above)
_____
_____
_____

5. _____(Rewrite from above)
_____
_____
_____

After rewriting the top five again (below), I went back and wrote why it is an absolute *must* that I either eliminate or change each thing that has adversely affected me and the people in my life and why not changing will continue to cause great pain.

1. _____(Rewrite from above)
_____
_____
_____

2. _____(Rewrite from above)
_____
_____
_____

3. _____(Rewrite from above)
_____
_____
_____

4. _____(Rewrite from above)
_____
_____
_____

5. _____(Rewrite from above)
_____

_____
_____

The change I can make *now* that will help me to eliminate, change, or modify these negative things is:

_____
_____
_____
_____.

Through this process, I have learned that by utilizing the *right* people and things, I can increase my chances of success in eliminating the negative things in my life. (This assistance is called *leverage*.) By gaining leverage, I will have the support and encouragement to deal with the things that have been damaging me, impeding my growth, and affecting my family and friends negatively.

To help me gain leverage, I will reach out to the people listed below:

Name: _____ Relationship to me:_____
Name: _____ Relationship to me:_____
Name: _____ Relationship to me:_____

I can utilize things, such as motivational programs and exercise equipment, which will also give me leverage. These things are:

_____
_____
_____
_____.

I commit to doing the following in beginning to address and eliminate these things in my life that have caused me pain:

Within the next month I will:

_____
_____
_____
_____.

Within the next week, I will:

_____
_____
_____
_____.

Brutally Honest Life Management Journal

I will immediately:

_____
_____
_____
_____

This exercise has truly motivated me to eliminate these problems. I feel better now that I know I can—on my own in some areas and with leverage in others—eliminate or modify these problems. I have a whole different perspective and outlook. I feel I am getting very close to your Core.

After analyzing these ten problematic issues, and applying the positive tools above, I would now rate them as follows on the same pain scale I used earlier:

_____
_____
_____
_____
_____
_____
_____
_____
_____
_____
_____

> *The best thing to give your enemy is forgiveness; to an opponent, tolerance; to a friend, your heart; to your children, a good example; to a father, difference; to your mother, conduct that will make her proud of you; to yourself, respect; to all men, charity.*
> —Francis Balfour

Soul's Core: The Arrival

Perception can become reality. I am seeing that my thoughts, and how I direct them, can radically change how I feel at times. By shifting the meaning that I attach to these perceptions, I can change my attitude from poor to focused—or anything that I choose.

In the past, when asked about my future, I would often parrot back a list of goals I wanted to achieve: making a difference in the world, becoming a millionaire, owning multiple homes, having a great family, creating a charity, and the like. It felt good telling this to people, as I truly did feel that I wanted those things and would achieve them. The problem lay in the fact that after the conversation waned, and life continued at its frantic pace, I lost sight of many of these goals. While admirable, these goals were only words.

> *Words without action do not yield results.*
> —Gregory LaMonaca

Soul, having joined you on a tour of my past and present, I feel a new sense of clarity. The difference this time around is that with your help I feel that I am inextricably aligned and attached to you. I feel that my focus is at a higher level than ever before. I never thought before today about how important my past has been in shaping my beliefs, attitudes, and outlook. I know now that I could not have taken the necessary steps to plan my future without first examining my past, deciding what has been helpful and hurtful, and taking whatever steps were necessary to move forward with my life. I can see now why many of the other self-help materials I have used in the past failed to work. They immediately had me attempt to "do as they did" in an effort to replicate *their* results. They did this without allowing me to first analyze *my* past and assess *my* present before moving forward. This then resulted in futile and frustrating attempts to be like them. You have taught me that I am different, unique, and wonderful. I must design *my* future based solely upon what works for *me*. While I can—and should—learn from as many different sources as I can; in the end, I should pick and choose only those attributes that can assist me in getting where I need to go.

Brutally Honest Life Management Journal

I have, for the first time, been totally Brutally Honest with myself. I have shed life's stereotypes and have truly looked into and arrived at my Core. Here at the Soul's Core, I feel free. I am not ashamed of things I have been holding back. I have honestly assessed my past, determined what may have been holding me back, and have not relied on all of life's "marketing" efforts to convert me into something society wants me to be. I am now ready to honestly, openly, and without reservation, determine and forge a path to the rest of my life.

Here at the Soul's Core, the weight of the world has been lifted from me. I can see that I have lived my life based on what others wanted me to be. I know now who in my life has empowered me, and those who have impeded my getting to know you.

Now, if you will allow me, I want to fully, and without reservation, take the next steps. Through this journey, you have allowed me to explore my innermost thoughts and

> *You cannot dream yourself into character;*
> *you must hammer and forge one yourself.*
> —James A. Froude

being. You have helped me to determine what matters most to me. I have made mistakes along the way, and you have not judged me. I was able to tell you my most embarrassing secrets, which I have never told anyone. By holding back in the past and not telling others how I truly felt, I was going through life wearing shackles. While I was perhaps putting forth the right energy, I was not able to move forward because I was holding myself back.

You promised that when I reached your Core I would have a better understanding of what I needed to do to begin the rest of my life. You were right. Armed with this extra knowledge and clarity about my past and present, I am now ready to forge forward along the road to empowerment and create my compelling future. I have a newfound level of excitement.

Here, at Soul's Core, I have finally arrived at the bottom of the Breakdown stage. I have established my baseline. I have completed my Net Life Statement. I now have an accurate assessment of where I am.

Through your intercession and guidance, you have taught me the value and importance of having someone assist me in getting to my desired outcome. In the journey downward to your Core, you were there every step of the way to hold my hand and keep me on track. Now that I am ready to move forward into the future, I would be honored if you would be my Brutally Honest coach.

As I embark on this journey, I know that there will be times when I lose focus, get upset, or simply become detoured. A coach is someone whom I can use to help keep me accountable and whom I will periodically call upon to discuss where I am on my path toward my Target Zones. I need you also to continue to motivate, inspire, and remind me of the importance of staying on track.

Now that I have found you, I don't want to lose you. Thank you in advance for being my Brutally Honest barometer as I start this journey.

Very Truly Yours,

_____

> *Most of the critical things in life, which become the starting points of human destiny, are the little things.*
> —Robert P. Smith

A Note on Discipline

Congratulations! If you have made it this far, you may be seeking some affirmation of your work. The rewards will come, but you must stay focused. What is discipline, and why does it seem to be so difficult to have a disciplined and ordered life (while still having fun)? Discipline is another tool that we can add to our Brutally Honest toolbox to help guide us through this wondrous journey called life.

There is no set clear-cut and steadfast definition of discipline as it applies to human nature. One hundred people will have one hundred different definitions of the term. But again, why is this idea of discipline so difficult to capture or verbalize, and why are there so many definitions? The answer to this is not nearly as hard as you may think. In fact it is right in front of us now and always has been. The truth is that discipline is so difficult for us to define, much less practice in our life, because it forces us to be Brutally Honest with ourselves. Discipline is relative and personal to each of us.

> *Little drops of water,*
> *little grains of sand,*
> *make the mighty ocean*
> *and the pleasant land;*
> *so the little minutes,*
> *humble though they be,*
> *make the mighty ages*
> *of eternity.*
> —Julia A. Fletcher Carney

Brutally Honesty is the art of looking deep within ourselves and getting to the core of what and who we really are.

Let's take a brief moment to answer a few basic questions.

1. Do you wake up each day at the same time (relative to the particular day of the week)? _____
2. When you awake, do you have a certain routine that you follow? _____
3. Do you have a career that you go to each day, and do you go with the intent to perform to the best of your ability? _____
4. Do you have a regular fitness routine? _____
5. Do you eat and drink in moderation? _____
6. Are you at a weight that is healthy and complimentary to your lifestyle and physical abilities?_____
7. If you are in a relationship (spouse/significant other/children) are you committed to making it work on a daily basis? _____
8. On average do you go to sleep at the same time? _____

9. Do you regularly contribute to charity and/or donate your time? _____
10. Do you inspire others to be the best that they can be? _____
11. Do you mentor others? _____

Did you answer yes to all of the above? Were you Brutally Honest with yourself, or did you fill in the blanks with the expected answer—or worse, the answer you know is not true but that you continue to make yourself believe is true? That may sound a bit harsh, but we are trying to overemphasize the point that until you get Brutally Honest with yourself, you will never achieve your full potential. Unless you start getting Brutally Honest with yourself you will continue to cheat yourself. Do you truly understand what that last sentence meant? *You will cheat yourself.* You may fool others into thinking something else, but at the end of the day, it is you that must live with your thoughts and decisions.

Being a disciplined person is not some impossible quest. It really starts with a simple desire to take charge of your life. Today is the day you take charge. Empowerment is nothing more than taking responsibility and following through. We'll start by helping you empower yourself. Let's get disciplined!

Many people are not disciplined. Few realize that the real issue of discipline is not about whether you are physically tough, but whether you are mentally tough. Do you control your mind, or does your mind control you? We think this point is extremely important. Every time we slip backwards it is because we have not controlled our minds. The fact is that your mind wants you to control it, and it will support any thoughts you have. Unfortunately, your mind will support negative as well as positive thoughts.

For example,, have you ever heard a parent say to a child, "You are bad"? I am sure you have, and maybe you have said this to someone as well. Perhaps the child was acting badly at that moment, but were they really bad? The answer, of course, is no; but to the child this begins to create an anchor in his or her young and developing brain that tells the child he or she is bad, when in fact the child may just have been tired and in need of rest. I am not saying that you should not discipline your children, but keep in mind that *words* have tremendous power and tremendous effect.

Here is a great exercise that will really make you think! For one week, think

> *Life is made up, not of great sacrifices or duties, but of little things, in which smiles and kindness and small obligations, given habitually, are what win and preserve the heart and secure comfort.*
> —Sir Humphrey Davy

Brutally Honest Life Management Journal

about everything you say about yourself and rephrase it in a positive way. For example: If you make a mistake do not say, "Wow, I am stupid for doing that!" Instead say, "Perhaps that was not the best thing for me to do, but I have truly learned from my error." If you would like to "supercharge" your effort, try writing in your journal the things you caught yourself saying that were negative and how you changed the words to make them a motivating statement. Give it a try, and you will be amazed at how you feel at the end of the week. Have fun with it, and notice if you consistently have negative thoughts about yourself.

Stage II:
Creating Your Compelling Future
Brutally Honest Target Zones

So, how did that feel? So far, through this process, you were able to engage your soul with a letter in a way that was previously unimaginable. As promised, there are no grades, as you are the ultimate judge. You, and only you, unless you choose otherwise, decide how you did, and how you feel.

Have you ever woken up from a dream, feeling that you actually were there, living the moment in which you were scared to death, elated, or experiencing some other strong emotion? If the dream was scary, you awake feeling relieved that it was not real. On the other hand, if it was a joyous dream, you awake feeling upset that it was not really true. Is it possible to convert these dreams into reality? Dreaming the big dream is a way to program your mind for success through the process of defining, engaging, and accomplishing your individual Target Zones.

Have you ever sat back and observed children at play? What did you see? Children dream the big dream every day. They fantasize about being Barbie, warriors, G.I. Joe, Transformers, or any one of the endless creations they can conjure up. They chase each other in the fields, slide aimlessly down playground slides, and play fight with their brothers and sisters.

Why aren't adults the same way? What happens to us as we get older? The answer lies with the same societal conditioning that you came to know in the Breakdown Phase. As we get older, society, peer pressure, and the multitude of other suggestors attack us from the moment we wake until the time we go to bed. We are conditioned to be, act, dress, and look like what society tells us is acceptable. To fit in, we must wear the newest fad jeans, speak like our friends, and hang with the in crowd. As life evolves, without consciously knowing it at times, we are taught how and what to be.

So the question we have for you is this: Is it possible to recondition your conditioning? Sure it is! With the added focus and clarity that you now have, you are ready to set your sights high.

> *Every noble acquisition is attended with its risk; he who fears to encounter the one must not expect to obtain either.*
> —Pietro Metastasio

Creating Brutally Honest Target Zones

> *Jim*
>
> In time I learned to deal with Mom's passing and move on. I replaced the nights of recklessness with days and nights of thinking and planning about how I would become a millionaire. I have always believed that if you make a goal and you tell everyone you are going to do it, you will. So I told all of the people around me that I was going to be a millionaire by age thirty. Then I set off on a very narrowly focused path to achieve this goal. At that time I did not know that I was developing my Brutally Honest Target Zones. I just was going by my instinct and sheer determination to be someone.
>
> Many people laughed or thought I was kidding when I told them of my goal. Let's face it—there were not a lot of millionaires coming out of Middletown, Pennsylvania, at the time and certainly not many that had no place to live and barely enough to eat! It really did not matter to me, as I have always had a loner streak and the ability to not care about what anyone else thought but me. I finally reached my goal of becoming a millionaire with the successful initial public offering of Ulticom. I missed my time goal by a couple of years, but the journey helped to shape the person I am today. (I consequently gave up many millions two years later to become a father and a good husband, but that is another story.)
>
> The important thing to remember is that you need a plan. You need to develop goals and target zones and interconnecting paths to reach your goals; and just when you think you have reached your goal do another plan and set new ones. Have fun with your life and live it the way you want. Remember: if you say you can, you can; and if you say you can't, then you can't. It is that simple.

A Ten-Year Day-in-the-Life Statement

Achieving your Brutally Honest Target Zones begins with a vision. Not just any vision, but a compelling vision. How does this process happen? How do you go about creating a compelling future? How can you ensure that when you create your Target Zones this time, it will be different than when you simply stated your goals previously?

You know the difference lies in your perception. Your soul taught you to be uninhibited, open, and honest in assessing your past and present.

Now that you have found your Soul's Core, it's time to supercharge things to help you achieve your compelling future. Your soul is now ready to be your ally and coach to help guide you through the rest of the process. Engage your soul once again, and ask its help. It's time to write your compelling future.

DATE, 20___

Dear Soul:

I first want to again sincerely thank you for allowing me to get to know you at your deepest level, your Core. You guided me through the very difficult Breakdown Phase, and I have begun to take control of my life. Now, as I embark on the first step toward the rest of my life, I ask for your assistance again to coach me through the process. I need you to be Brutally Honest with me, and I apologize in advance for any resistance I may still give you.

Likewise, I commit to you again, my coach, that I will continue on this journey in the same unfettered and unrestricted style. I have also learned humility in understanding that there will be bumps in the road. Help me through these bumps and guide me in this most important journey.

To begin the process of creating my compelling future, I will start with describing a day in my life, ten years from now. To do this I will describe my day from the time I wake until the time I go to bed. Keep in mind that this day represents my most ideal day. It will describe all areas of my life including:

- family;
- friends;
- finances;
- where I'll be living;
- whom I'll be living with;
- what I'll see when I look out my window;
- career;
- emotions;
- spirituality;
- health;

Brutally Honest Life Management Journal

- hobbies; and
- anything else my heart desires.

This is a Brutally Honest Free Flow of my mind, allowing me to write the first thing that comes to mind. I know you will remind me that I am not being graded, and as such, there is no wrong answer. Here, I will let myself be a child again and write down my dreams. This is how I want my ultimate life to be ten years from now. The date is: _____

_____ (ten years from today), and my dreams for this time are:

_____
_____
_____
_____
_____
_____
_____
_____
_____
_____
_____
_____
_____

That was incredible, and most of all, fun. It was great to allow my mind to free flow and flood with whimsical fancy. I had to catch myself a few times as I was writing what I thought people would want to read, as opposed to what I truly wanted. Once I shifted fully into this mode and wrote everything according to _____ _____ (insert your first name), amazing things happened. How wonderful it will be to actually achieve these goals. I am anxious to keep the train rolling and convert the whimsical fancy into reality. It is great creating my own, real-life reality series.

After this initial free flow of information, my vision is that of a black-and-white snapshot of my future. It's a great first start, but I am ready to move beyond black and white—to color.

> *True politeness is perfect ease and freedom. It simply consists in treating others just as you love to be treated yourself.*
> —Philip Dormer Stanhope Chesterfield

Target Zones versus Goals

Soul, during my life, there have been times when I felt that I was basically wandering aimlessly from day to day with no clear direction. As I told you before, I had goals for myself, but I never actually had a detailed, written, plan on how to get there. This time, I will be creating Target Zones to aid me in my quest. Many self-help and time-management programs demand very regimented to-do lists that must be created and followed. Many of these programs are excellent but they require a regimented personality to make them work.

If you aim for the bull's-eye, you are significantly better off than the individual who refuses to pick up the bow; however, even that person is better off than the one who does not even know where the bow is. My point is that I want to shoot toward the target. I have the bow in my hand. I want to pull back on the cord, look at the center of the bull's-eye, and have the confidence to let go. I know now that, once I release, I am on track to hit the bull's-eye. On my first attempt, I may not make it to the center, or the first ring, or even the second, but I revel in the power that accompanies the process.

I know that to make the vision more vivid, realistic, and believable, I must begin to convert the vision into reality in my mind. I want it to get to a point where I can taste it, feel it, be it. As we learned, many of history's greatest figures possessed the magical secret of the Law of Attraction. As with the dreams that appear real, our minds cannot tell the difference between reality and dreams. This is why a person wakes up in a cold sweat after a scary dream. It follows then, that if I program my mind for the successful attainment of the compelling future that I just wrote about, it will begin to program all parts of my conscious and subconscious to actually attain my vision.

Brutally Honest Target Zones

As I learned from my past, everybody is different insofar as what categories are important to him or her. There are a lot of categories that make up one's life, including health, finances, spirituality, career, relationships, emotions, and fun.

I have given this a lot of thought, and after reviewing the Brutally Honest Free Flow that I did in my Ten-Year Day-in-My-Life exercise, I can see the following categories in my life (in no particular order):

_____

_____

_____
_____
_____
_____

This vision includes some or all of the categories or subcategories that I included in my Net Life Statement, specifically:

_____
_____
_____
_____
_____
_____

After thinking about this more fully, I can see additional categories that were not included in the Ten-Year Day-in-the-Life exercise, specifically:

_____
_____
_____
_____
_____
_____

I'm sure I failed to consider other categories, but these represent the major ones in my life ten years from now. After ranking all the categories, I can see that one category in particular is my highest priority in the future.

When I carefully look at the categories I created, I can start to see similarities amongst a number of them. These similar categories are Target Zones. For example, my children, spouse, and parents are all very important to me. I may call this set of categories "family." Likewise, I may have listed "becoming a millionaire," "investing in stocks," and "buying real estate." These may be linked together under the Target Zone called "finances."

After looking at my lists of categories above, I have broken them down into the following Brutally Honest Target Zones with the rank of each category written next to it:

Target Zone:_____
Categories:
_____

Brutally Honest Life Management Journal

_____
_____
_____
_____
_____

Target Zone: _____
Categories:
_____
_____
_____
_____
_____

Target Zone: _____
Categories:
_____
_____
_____
_____
_____

Target Zone: _____
Categories:
_____
_____
_____
_____
_____

Target Zone: _____
Categories:
_____
_____
_____
_____
_____

This act of finding common associations has helped me group and conceptualize the many categories in my life into easy-to-remember Brutally Honest Target

Zones.

Seeing each Brutally Honest Target Zone written out has prompted me to think of more categories within each Zone, so I have filled in the remaining blanks with additional categories. Of course I can certainly have as many Target Zones and categories as I want but will focus in on five Target Zones for now.

> *People never improve unless they look to some standard or example higher and better than themselves.*
> —Tyron Edwards

Now that I have broken down each of my categories in Brutally Honest Target Zones, I have rewritten just the five Target Zones below along with their rank from one to five :

_____
_____
_____
_____

Breaking down the various categories into Brutally Honest Target Zones has forced me for the first time to combine all of the similar parts of my compelling vision. Creating these Brutally Honest Target Zones, as opposed to just goals has given me a better sense of clarity about my desired outcomes and the ease of getting there. By creating various targets in the future, I have begun to compile the building blocks for the attainment of my vision.

Soul, you have previously helped me learn about, and get in touch with my "onboard computer system," which is called my reticular activating system or RAS. I know now that my RAS is like the world's most powerful global positioning system (GPS). Much like the way a GPS is used to pinpoint any location in the world with incredible accuracy, so too will my RAS guide me toward my Brutally Honest Target Zones.

When we began this journey and before I found your Core, I could not understand why, if we are all born with this most powerful internal GPS, we do not all achieve incredible success? Shouldn't we all be rich, powerful, and successful? Wouldn't it follow that we should be living in a world filled with superhuman beings, all of whom have achieved incredible success and abundance?

You taught me that the answer did not lie in the fact that we all have this ability. We all have a RAS that was installed in each of us by our creator. The difference lies in how each unit was programmed initially, adjusted over time, and utilized by the

Brutally Honest Life Management Journal

recipient. By examining my past, I discovered how my RAS was programmed based upon my first thoughts. I saw that this was done initially by my parents, relatives, friends, and everyone I came in contact with as I grew up. Every waking second found millions of bits of data flooding into my body through all of my senses, which were constantly refining, adjusting, and modifying my RAS. The sum total of all of this continues to shape my personality today. All of the people, places, and things that influence me—consciously and unconsciously—continue to modify my RAS.

Advertisers attempt to modify my RAS through suggestions about how I should act and dress and what I should eat and drink. My family, friends, co-workers, and everybody I come in contact with add to the programming, both good and bad.

In the end, however, you taught me that it is I who ultimately has the power to control the gates to my RAS I can *choose* what information to use and what to dismiss. Through your guidance in my past, I learned how my present was created, influenced, and shaped. I learned what was good for me (empowering) and what was bad for me (disempowering). With this conscious knowledge in hand, I am now better equipped to truly define my own future. I know what influences I should dismiss and which I should embrace in planning my Brutally Honest Target Zones and in creating my Brutally Honest Life Management System

With these ten-year Brutally Honest Target Zones clearly in sight, I now will try to focus in on the bull's-eye by gaining a clearer vision and setting the arrow in flight. I know that just creating the target does not ensure success. However, by doing this exercise and committing these targets to you *in writing*, I have begun to be accountable to you, my coach. It feels great!

At this point, I have my ten-year Brutally Honest Target Zones, along with their categories. I arrived at these by having fun and free-flowing my compelling vision of the future. I have chosen ten years as a time frame, as it is well into the future and allows a realistic amount of time for my vision to be realized. It might seem that there are exceptions to this, for example, a person who is over one hundred or someone who has been diagnosed with a terminal illness with little time to live, but in these cases, creating a compelling future is even more imperative.

By creating the various Brutally Honest Target Zones with their associated categories, I have begun to colorize my future. If I stopped now, while I would certainly feel a better sense of certainty, it would soon revert back to uncertainty. I must take the steps necessary to move forward, in order for me to reach Utopia,. I know that every step I take, however small, brings me closer toward the attainment of each of my Brutally Honest Target Zones.

> *It may serve as comfort to us on all our calamities and afflictions, that he who loses anything and gets wisdom by it, is a gainer by the loss.*
> —Sir Roger L'Estrange

Blasting Off to Utopia

Utopia is the never-ending pursuit of excellence measured by the satisfaction of living life to the fullest.
—*Gregory LaMonaca*

This may sound like an illusive thing to shoot for given that the pursuit is, by definition, "never-ending." But Utopia itself is never-ending. While we all have our own beliefs as to what happens to our physical and/or spiritual bodies after death, we must also create our own individual belief system of what is happening to us *while we are still alive*. As I have learned, Soul, I am in control of my onboard computer, and as such, I am choosing excellence, as well as committing today to move toward my personal Utopia. The difference this time is that I know that I have you, my coach, to assist me in my journey.

You have assisted me in creating my top five Brutally Honest Target Zones with all of the various categories that fall within each one. I then ranked them to differentiate my primary target from my lower priorities. These rankings helped me separate and visualize what it is truly essential for me to achieve, as opposed to a mere wishes or wants. After analyzing the categories I listed from my original Free Flow exercise, I have come to see that many of the categories and things that I listed are not truly things that I want, but instead were idealistic and/or unreasonable.

I realize that while there is infinite abundance to seek (a bottomless well), there is a finite amount of time (a bucket of water) to devote to doing so. Thus it is important for me to utilize the water in my bucket in a way that is likely to help me get to my most important Brutally Honest Target Zones.

With you as my coach, I can sense that you are working behind the scenes, guiding every decision I make. You have taught me that each Brutally Honest Target Zone must be broken down into bite-size steps so that a plan can be put into effect to allow me to reach each target.

> *To know how to suggest is the art of teaching.*
> —Henri Frederick Amiel

Looking at each Brutally Honest Target Zone, I can see a pathway to its attainment through the utilization of vivid visualization. For each target, there are clear pathways that exist to take me from point A to point B. Creating and defining these pathways will make the difference between my success and failure. Clearly then, I will strive to create Brutally Honest Success Pathways.

As I saw by analyzing the various categories that were present within my Ten-Year Day-in-the-Life exercise, I could place them into Brutally Honest Target Zones. To move me along to attaining each Target Zone, I will have to create Brutally Honest Success Pathways, the roads that will bridge the gaps from where I am now to each Brutally Honest Target Zone. To help with this, I have listed each Brutally Honest Target Zone below and have written a compelling and concise vision statement encompassing the various categories within each Target Zone. This paragraph should be brief, powerful and dynamic. Next, I listed the top five (or fewer) outcomes that must occur ten years from now in order for me to hit each target. An example is below.

Target Zone: family

I am married to my life partner, the person with whom I share, learn, and love and who accompanies me through the rest of my life. We have two wonderful children and together form a dynamic, stable, and loving family. My parents are an amazing and important part of my life and spend a lot of time nurturing and guiding their grandchildren.

Necessary outcomes ten years from now:
- I am married.
- My spouse and I have two children.
- My parents are alive.
- We spend time as a family solidifying the family unit.
- My spouse's and my parents spend time with their grandchildren.

By doing this, I can see that there are things on the list that I can control and things that I cannot. For this exercise, I want to only list those things that I can control and that can be measured. These should be things that *must* happen ten years from now in order to achieve my desired outcome. So, for the example above, the list should only contain:

- I am married.
- My spouse and I have two children.
- We spend time as a family solidifying the family unit.

I eliminated "My parents are alive," since I cannot control this. I also noticed that two of the outcomes are similar and can be merged together, namely:

Brutally Honest Life Management Journal

- We spend time as a family solidifying the family unit.
- My spouse's and my parents spend time with their grandchildren.

These two can be combined as follows:

- Our family (me, my spouse, our two children, and our parents) spends time together solidifying the family unit.

The necessary outcome list now reads as follows:
- I am married.
- My spouse and I have two children.
- Our family (me, my spouse, our two children, and our parents) spends time together solidifying the family unit.

While I said that I can have as many Target Zones as I wish, I have chosen to focus on my top five only. While the other ones are important, I want to concentrate the "water in my bucket" on the top five only. I know I can always do this same exercise with the remaining Brutally Honest Target Zones or add as many as I want later. You have taught me that if I dilute my focus by concentrating on too many things at once, I will reduce the likelihood of reaching the most important Brutally Honest Target Zones. Go forward with the lessons that we have learned together. I remain here to assist you throughout your journey

Using this model as my guide, here are my results:

Target Zone 1: _____

Compelling and Concise Vision Statement (ten years in the future):
_____
_____
_____
_____

Necessary outcomes ten years from now:

1._____
_____
_____
_____

2._____
_____

3._____

4._____

5._____

Target Zone 2: _____
Compelling and Concise Vision Statement (ten years in the future):
_____
_____

Necessary outcomes ten years from now:
1._____

2._____

3._____

4._____

Brutally Honest Life Management Journal

5. _____

Target Zone 3: _____
Compelling and Concise Vision Statement (ten years in the future):

Jim

I had just received my first semester grades at Capitol College where I was studying engineering. To my great joy, I had received a 4.0—straight A's. The pride I felt was incredible; engineering is a very tough major, and the chances of graduating with honors or even high honors is difficult, to say the least. This was also a turning point for me because it showed me that it was even possible to get such high grades. So I made a plan to get straight A's and graduate with highest honors.

An important part of achieving this goal came from my having an absolutely clear picture of what I would need to do and what it would look like while I was doing it and also from identifying clear and measurable points to make sure I was on track. One semester, I received a B in my digital circuit design course—I was devastated. I felt this could not happen to me because it was not in my plan. In the end, I received one more B (in Chemistry) and ended up graduating magna cum laude.

As you plan out your next ten years or so, make sure you truly know what your driving force is. Create your compelling future and be ready to adjust your plan when necessary. My own driving force was the fact that, the day I graduated, I needed a job to buy food and shelter. That is a pretty big motivator. The reality was that companies viewed very high grade point averages as a reflection of what types of workers students would be, and I was not leaving anything to chance. I had no safety net. There was no going back to Mom and Dad's house.

Take this time to begin to write out your awesome future.

Necessary outcomes ten years from now:

1._____
_____
_____
_____

2._____
_____
_____
_____

3._____
_____
_____
_____

4._____
_____
_____
_____

5._____
_____
_____
_____

Target Zone 4: _____
Compelling and Concise Vision Statement (ten years in the future):
_____
_____
_____

Necessary outcomes ten years from now:
1._____
_____
_____

2._____
_____
_____

Brutally Honest Life Management Journal

3._____

4._____

5._____

Target Zone 5: _____
Compelling and Concise Vision Statement (ten years in the future):

Necessary outcomes ten years from now:
1._____

2._____

3._____

4._____

5._____

> *No man is so foolish but he may sometimes find another good counsel, and no man so wise that he may not easily err if he takes no other counsel than his own. He that is taught only by himself has a fool for a master.*
> —Ben Johnson

You now have your top five Brutally Honest Target Zones for ten years from now, along with the corresponding necessary outcomes, which *must* take place for them to become reality. You should feel wonderful because you have taken the first real steps toward making your vision a reality. We must also add that while we are here to coach and guide you through the process, *you* have to take the necessary steps to secure your future. You must have the tenacity to stay the course. This has not been an easy process. You should feel incredibly proud of your accomplishments. You are continuing to separate yourself from the majority of the world, those who simply subsist and go from one day to the next with no clear vision or pathway to the future. Through this process, you continue to pave your Brutally Honest Success Pathways, one brick at a time.

You now should have a clear vision of your ideal life ten years from now. You also have a vivid, colorful snapshot of each of your five Brutally Honest Target Zones. It is critical to your ultimate success that this vision always remains clear. We know, however, that while it would be ideal to be able to have this happen, life will inevitably throw you many curveballs. You will be inundated at times with many stressful situations that will challenge you. Illness, death, job stress, family problems, and the like will at times do their best to derail you and place barriers in the way of your Brutally Honest Success Pathways.

> *It is through our failures that success seeds are planted. It is through the recognition of and learning from our failures that these seeds are fertilized, and it is through the willingness to take corrective future actions that abundant trees reign free.*
> —Gregory LaMonaca

recordings, and DVDs on personal excellence, investing, and the like. I consistently improve my knowledge base by studying these materials.

Do you see the difference between the two entries? Which one is more likely to keep you on track? The next step in this process is below.

Based on the paragraph above, what are the top five things that need to happen in five years for you to reach this target, and why?

1) I set up automatic payroll deductions with automatic investment.

I will have money automatically withdrawn so I will be conditioned to not miss this money. I also won't forget to deduct and invest or put it off. This will ensure that I pay myself first and dollar cost average. Over time, my net worth, will continue to grow automatically.

2) I have an emergency living fund.

I will have an emergency fund set up to protect me in the event of an unexpected financial or personal setback (loss of job or health setbacks). I will ensure that I have all of the appropriate insurance as well (life, disability, homeowners, automobile, umbrella policy, etc.). I will consult with my Brutally Honest board of directors to ensure that I have the right policies in effect to protect my family.

3) I have a diversified collection of assets.

I know that all investments go up and down over time. To protect me during these inevitable (and healthy) corrections, I will spread my risk out over various types of investments (real estate, stocks, bonds, cash, etc.) and within each type, I will further diversify among different sectors (retail, industrial, energy, etc.) and allocate appropriately based upon my existing risk tolerance.

4) I have a Brutally Honest board of directors.

I will focus on what I do best while having a team of experts, who are the best at what they do, to advise me and assist me. This will ensure that I stay on track to achieving my Brutally Honest Target Zones.

5) I expand my education and financial literacy.

I have gradually and consistently expanded my personal library of books, audio recordings, and DVDs in the area of personal excellence, finances, taxes, real estate, and many other areas. I commit to continued improvement by furthering my personal education. I have a better understanding of my net worth, and I am better equipped to both guide and interact with my Brutally Honest Board of directors.

Now it's your turn. The following exercises will solidify your Brutally Honest Success Pathway by adding indestructible bricks and adding layers to your Brutally Honest suit of armor to deflect life's challenges.

> *When trying to help or communicate your position to others, you can't keep pounding on a steel door with your fists. It will cause pain and frustration and exert a lot of energy. Instead, use minimal energy by finding a key to the door to unlock the roadblock with a simple twist of the wrist.*
> —Gregory LaMonaca

Brutally Honest Life Management Journal

Five-Year Target Zones

Ten-Year Target Zone 1: _____
_____
_____

    What needs to happen in five years for you to be on track to hitting this target?
_____
_____
_____
_____
_____

    Based on the paragraph above, what are the top five things that need to happen in five years for you to reach this target?

1) _____
    Why? _____
_____
_____
_____
_____

2) _____
    Why? _____
_____
_____
_____
_____

3) _____
    Why? _____
_____
_____
_____

4) _____
    Why? _____
_____

_____
_____
_____

5) _____
    Why? _____
_____
_____
_____
_____

    Although you may be well-intentioned and focused, there will be obstacles that life throws in your path as you move down your Brutally Honest Success Pathways. You can pretend that these things will not happen, or you can prepare now to be ready for them. We don't have to even ask what your choice is.

    List five obstacles that could impede your attainment of this five-year target:

1) _____
2) _____
3) _____
4) _____
5) _____
    Why might these obstacles occur?
_____
_____
_____
_____
_____
_____
_____
_____
_____
_____
_____

    How could they adversely affect you?
_____
_____
_____
_____

Are there things you can do today to minimize the chances of these obstacles occurring, or are they outside of your control? _____

_____

_____

_____

_____

Remind yourself now that no matter how much you plan, there will be things that you simply *cannot* control. Therefore to worry about these things would simply be a waste of energy and time and would only cause unnecessary stress and anxiety. You should devote your energy and attention to those things that you *can* control.

When analyzing the present during the Brutally Honest Net Life Statement exercise, you discovered that you could increase your chances of success by utilizing the *right* people and things (leverage) and eliminating the negative things in your life that could impede you. By gaining leverage, you gain support, encouragement, and empowerment over those things that had previously damaged you and impeded your growth.

To help you gain leverage in ensuring your targets are on track, list the people whom you will reach out to over the next five years. Also list *why* these people are important to assisting you in achieving your target.

Person: _____

    Why? _____

_____

_____

_____

_____

Person: _____

    Why? _____

_____

_____

_____

_____

Person: _____

    Why? _____

_____
_____
_____
_____

Person: _____
    Why? _____
_____
_____
_____
_____

    Next, list things you can utilize to help you, such as motivational programs and exercise equipment that will give you added leverage, and why they will help you.

Thing: _____
    Why? _____
_____
_____
_____
_____

Thing: _____
    Why? _____
_____
_____
_____
_____

Thing: _____
    Why? _____
_____
_____
_____
_____

Thing: _____
    Why? _____
_____
_____
_____
_____

Brutally Honest Life Management Journal

> *Not in novelty but in habit and custom do we find the greatest pleasure.*
> —Raymond Radiguet

Lastly, for this Target Zone, write a one-paragraph statement that will uplift you and compel you to achieve this five-year target.

_____
_____
_____
_____
_____
_____
_____

Ten-Year Target Zone 2:
_____
_____

What needs to happen in five years for you to be on track to hitting this target?
_____
_____
_____
_____
_____
_____

Based on the paragraph above, what are the top five things that need to happen in five years for you to reach this target, and why?

1) _____
   Why? _____
   _____
   _____
   _____
   _____

2) _____
   Why? _____
   _____
   _____

3) _____
   Why? _____

4) _____
   Why? _____

5) _____
   Why? _____

Jim

My life has been a series of obstacles and plans to get over those obstacles. I have a fundamental belief that if you are maintaining or going laterally, you are falling behind. This is engrained in my brain, and I don't need to think about it. I naturally judge my plan based on if I am making forward progress.

One of the absolute keys is to be as specific in mapping out your plan as you possibly can. When you believe your plan is complete, step away from it and look at it with fresh eyes later. Share your plan with others. Let them shoot holes in it, and maybe one or two of their thoughts will be helpful. But always remain true to your plan and your ideals.

One day in seventh-grade algebra class, my teacher made a point of telling me that I was an oaf and that I would never understand mathematics. (I will not

> name this teacher because I do not want to embarrass her.) Her words hurt me, and for a while I went into a math death spiral. It got so bad that at one point I was not going to be able to continue to play sports because of my poor grades. I was given the choice to go into remedial math or continue in algebra. I chose to stay the course and prove the teacher wrong. I developed a plan, which included asking an attractive young lady to help me understand math, and the rest is history. Success in electrical engineering, a field based on abstract mathematics, is how I initially found financial success.
>
> I often think about that teacher and wonder what she ever did with her life. Although not by design, her belittling me actually made me stronger. Make sure you have a clear plan and stick to it, no matter who tells you that you can't do it. Believe in yourself, and make your future what you want it to be.

List five obstacles that could impede your attainment of this five-year target.

1) _____
2) _____
3) _____
4) _____
5) _____

Why might these obstacles occur?

_____
_____
_____
_____
_____

How could they adversely affect you?

_____
_____
_____
_____

Are there things you can do today to minimize the chances of these obstacles occurring, or are they outside of your control? _____
_____
_____

List people who can help you reach this five-year target and state *why* each is important.

Person: _____
   Why? _____
_____
_____
_____
_____
_____

Person: _____
   Why? _____
_____
_____
_____
_____
_____

Person: _____
   Why? _____
_____
_____
_____
_____
_____

Person: _____
   Why? _____
_____
_____
_____
_____
_____

Next, list things you can utilize to help you, such as motivational programs and exercise equipment that will give you added leverage, and why they will help you.

Brutally Honest Life Management Journal

> *One loses all the time which he might employ to better purpose.*
> —Jean Jacques Rousseau

Thing: _____
   Why? _____
_____
_____
_____
_____

Thing: _____
   Why? _____
_____
_____
_____
_____

Thing: _____
   Why? _____
_____
_____
_____
_____

Thing: _____
   Why? _____
_____
_____
_____
_____

Lastly, for this Target Zone, write a one-paragraph statement that will uplift you and compel you to achieve this five-year target.

_____
_____
_____
_____
_____

Ten-Year Target Zone 3:
_____
_____

What needs to happen in five years for you to be on track to hitting this target?
_____
_____
_____
_____
_____
_____

Based on the paragraph above, what are the top five things that need to happen in five years for you to reach this target, and why?

1) _____
   Why? _____
_____
_____
_____

2) _____
   Why? _____
_____
_____
_____

3) _____
   Why? _____
_____
_____
_____

4) _____
   Why? _____
_____
_____
_____

5) _____
    Why? _____
_____
_____
_____

    List five obstacles that could impede your attainment of this five-year target.

1) _____
2) _____
3) _____
4) _____
5) _____
    Why might these obstacles occur?:
_____
_____
_____
_____
_____
_____

How could they adversely affect you?
_____
_____
_____
_____
_____

    Are there things you can do today to minimize the chances of these obstacles occurring, or are they outside of your control? _____
_____
_____
_____
_____

    List people who can help you reach this five-year target and state *why* each is important.

Person: _____
   Why? _____
_____
_____
_____
_____

Person: _____
   Why? _____
_____
_____
_____
_____

Person: _____
   Why? _____
_____
_____
_____
_____

Person: _____
   Why? _____
_____
_____
_____
_____

    Next, list things you can utilize to help you, such as motivational programs and exercise equipment that will give you added leverage, and why they will help you.

Thing: _____
   Why? _____
_____
_____
_____

Thing: _____
   Why? _____
_____
_____

Thing: _____
    Why? _____

Thing: _____
    Why? _____

    Lastly, for this Target Zone, write a one-paragraph statement that will uplift you and compel you to achieve this five-year target.

> *Too many wish to be happy before becoming wise.*
> —Madame Necker

Ten-Year Target Zone 4:

    What needs to happen in five years for you to be on track to hitting this target?

Based on the paragraph above, what are the top five things that need to happen in five years for you to reach this target, and why?

1) _____
   Why? _____

2) _____
   Why? _____

3) _____
   Why? _____

4) _____
   Why? _____

5) _____
   Why? _____

Brutally Honest Life Management Journal

List five obstacles that could impede your attainment of this five-year target.

1) _____
2) _____
3) _____
4) _____
5) _____

Why might these obstacles occur?

_____
_____
_____
_____
_____

How could they adversely affect you?

_____
_____
_____
_____
_____

Are there things you can do today to minimize the chances of these obstacles occurring, or are they outside of your control? _____

_____
_____
_____
_____

List people who can help you reach this five-year target and state *why* each is important.

Person: _____

Why? _____

_____
_____
_____

Person: _____

Why? _____
_____
_____
_____

Person: _____
   Why? _____
_____
_____
_____

Person: _____
   Why? _____
_____
_____

   Next, list things you can utilize to help you, such as motivational programs and exercise equipment that will give you added leverage, and why they will help you.

Thing: _____
   Why? _____
_____
_____
_____

Thing: _____
   Why? _____
_____
_____
_____

Thing: _____
   Why? _____
_____
_____
_____

Thing: _____
    Why? _____
_____
_____
_____

    Lastly, for this Target Zone, write a one-paragraph statement that will uplift you and compel you to achieve this five-year target:

_____
_____
_____
_____
_____
_____
_____

Ten-Year Target Zone 5: _____
_____

    What needs to happen in five years for you to be on track to hitting this target?

_____
_____
_____
_____
_____
_____

    Based on the paragraph above, what are the top five things that need to happen in five years for you to reach this target, and why?

1) _____
    Why? _____
_____
_____
_____

2) _____
    Why? _____
_____

3) _____
   Why? _____

4) _____
   Why? _____

5) _____
   Why? _____

List five obstacles that could impede your attainment of this five-year target.

1) _____
2) _____
3) _____
4) _____
5) _____

> *There is always hope in a man who actually and earnestly works. In idleness alone is there perpetual despair.*
> —Thomas Carlyle

Why might these obstacles occur?

_____
_____

Brutally Honest Life Management Journal

_____
_____
_____

How could they adversely affect you?
_____
_____
_____
_____

Are there things you can do today to minimize the chances of these obstacles occurring, or are they outside of your control? _____
_____
_____
_____

List people who can help you reach this five-year target and state *why* each is important.

Person: _____
    Why? _____
_____
_____
_____

Person: _____
    Why? _____
_____
_____
_____

Person: _____
    Why? _____
_____
_____
_____

Person: _____
   Why? _____
   _____
   _____
   _____

   Next, list things you can utilize to help you, such as motivational programs and exercise equipment that will give you added leverage, and why they will help you.

Thing: _____
   Why? _____
   _____
   _____
   _____

Thing: _____
   Why? _____
   _____
   _____
   _____

Thing: _____
   Why? _____
   _____
   _____
   _____

Thing: _____
   Why? _____
   _____
   _____
   _____

Brutally Honest Life Management Journal

Lastly, for this Target Zone, write a one-paragraph statement that will uplift you and compel you to achieve this five-year target.

_____
_____
_____
_____

Congratulations! You have now finished mapping out your five-year targets. How do you feel? Do you feel more empowered? You should. You have taken yet another step forward toward the attainment of your Brutally Honest Target Zones. You continue to separate yourself from the majority of the world, those who simply wish for success or make broad statements about their futures without taking any action. You are a doer. You are taking personal responsibility for your future. You continue to successfully lay down Success Bricks on your Brutally Honest Success Pathway.

> *It seems to me we can never give up longing and wishing while we are thoroughly alive. There are certain things we feel to be beautiful and good, and we must hunger after them.*
> —George Eliot

The Brutally Honest One-Year Zone of Excellence

> ### *Jim*
>
> "You're not worth the powder it would take to blow you to hell!" That was one of my father's favorite ways to let you know what he thought of you. I heard this many times growing up, in addition to "I wish you were never born." Dad sure had a way with words, and they weighed heavily on me growing up. My father has since passed, but I only found this out through family friends, as I had no contact with him after I turned eighteen.
>
> Some would say that my father was an obstacle. I choose to consider him a key motivator in my life. My father showed me what not to be. By setting up these mental (and sometimes physical) obstacles, he helped to make me tough. Now, I do not recommend this type of parenting, and I certainly do not use these techniques on my kids; but these experiences did teach me that I can overcome obstacles and move on.
>
> I work on a daily basis with my daughters to teach them the Brutally Honest way to overcome obstacles. I believe that a person will respond positively to steady encouragement. Obstacles will begin to look like challenges, and challenges will begin to look like opportunities for success.

Like a funnel, you are slowly narrowing in on your Brutally Honest Target Zones. With your ten- and five-year targets now in front of you, you are ready to continue on your journey by further refining your vision. We are getting down to crunch time. Remember when we started with your Ten-Year Day-in-the-Life Statement? It was like a dream at that point. You created a compelling vision of your future, and when you broke your vision down to five-year goals, it probably still felt like you were writing about a fictitious person in a story. Well, that story is now casting for someone to play the lead role. Guess who that person will be?

Your future is *now*. It's time to truly start fleshing out your ultimate vision by developing a highly attainable one-year target. This target, one year in the future, is called the Brutally Honest Zone of Excellence, a veil of excellence that is cloaked around you as you enter into this one-year arena. It's a giant bubble that is draped around you as you execute your plan; it is forgiving, flexible, and expandable. It

Brutally Honest Life Management Journal

allows you to learn as you go, make mistakes, and keep on track during the process. In the past, you have at times set out to achieve things that didn't go as planned. How did you handle these setbacks? Did others say, "I told you you couldn't do it" or other such statements that reinforced the setback? It's normal during these times to feel discouraged and disappointed. Did you give up or did you continue through the heat of the fire?

The Brutally Honest Zone of Excellence is an environment where you *can* and *will* make mistakes. Don't be afraid to take risks during this year. With no risk, there can be no reward. While we are not telling you to disregard discretion, we *are* telling you to expand your previous comfort zone into a Brutally Honest Zone of Comfort. In the past, you might have been reluctant to do this. You created a fictitious environment where you felt safe. As long as you stayed within that environment, you had no fear. When you occasionally ventured outside that area, your reticular activating system told you that you shouldn't be there because it had been programmed over the years to avoid risk. We learned why this occurred in the past. Society told your reticular activating system what your limits should be, which in turn convinced you that it was true.

But you're different now. Your reticular activating system has been reprogrammed for success. You venture forward this time with your RAS programmed to allow you to achieve and hit your Brutally Honest Target Zones. Your previous comfort zone has been

> *Great effects come of industry and perseverance; for audacity doth almost blind and mate the weaker sort of minds.*
> —Francis Bacon

radically expanded; you have a newfound willingness to venture out into this often scary, yet exhilarating, new world of possibilities. You would be a fool to disregard and not anticipate the risk of venturing outside your old comfort zone. That said, *calculated* risk should not be avoided, but embraced.

While we would all like to be certain about our futures, we know that this cannot happen. Do we not also need a little uncertainty? Why do we enjoy reading books? Don't we revel in the uncertainty of what is going to happen? Try this experiment and see what happens. The next time you're at the beach with someone who is relaxing on a chair reading a good novel, ask to see the book for a second, go to the last page, read the ending to them, and see how they react. Of course, this is just a facetious suggestion. If you do try this, you may also want to run as fast as you can when you're done! Obviously, if you were foolish enough to try this, you would be met with a very angry reaction. Why? because people read fiction to temporarily suspend reality—to be swept away into the magical and uncertain worlds that books take them into.

On the other hand, we also often read books that give us a sense of certainty. We read biographies of individuals we may already know about to reinforce the information that we have heard before. Why do we reread books again and again? We do this because it brings back feelings that we previously had that we want to relive. We relish this sense of certainty as we remind our reticular activating system about these good feelings.

As you move forward over the next year, take chances, make mistakes, and feel good about the process. You will periodically stumble, but you should focus on your outcomes. In your Brutally Honest Zone of Excellence you will not be critiqued by anyone other than yourself. Don't be afraid to keep expanding this veil of security; with each step forward you are expanding the veil exponentially. Know also that you are improving every step of the way as you head toward your Brutally Honest Target Zones! Don't ever forget that I am here with you to hold your hand as you venture outside your Brutally Honest Zone of Comfort.

As your Soul, and guide on this journey,

I will catch you if you fall …

… embrace you when you stumble, and …

… love you unconditionally during the journey.

Let's do it!

You must continue to remind your reticular activating system about what your mission is. Rewrite your ten-year Brutally Honest Target Zones below:

Target Zone 1: _____
Target Zone 2: _____
Target Zone 3: _____
Target Zone 4: _____
Target Zone 5: _____

One year from now, the date will be: _____, 20__.

Stare at this date for a minute. Do you realize just how close that date is? Think about where you were one year ago. A lot has happened in that short period. You have undoubtedly had your share of ups and downs. The year went by quickly, didn't it? As Anthony Robbins said, "The past does not equal the future." Let's keep the momentum you have made moving forward as we supercharge the next year.

Close your eyes for a moment. Taking into consideration your five Target Zones above, create a mental picture of where you will be one year in the future, incorporating all five targets. Do you like what you see? Jump into the picture. Embrace the image. Change it around; colorize it; feel, hear, smell, touch, and taste it. Once you are sure that the image in your head is exactly what you want, write a detailed summary of what you see below.

_____
_____
_____
_____
_____
_____
_____
_____
_____
_____
_____
_____
_____

Let's now break down each of the five Brutally Honest Target Zones to individually refine each one. Keep in mind that although the questions are similar to the ones that you have previously examined in assessing your five-year plan, it is critically important to break each one down further as you put together the following one-year plan. Each stroke of your pen throughout this journal builds an additional layer of strength within your Brutally Honest Veil of Comfort. Repetition and analysis will continue to strengthen your focus and commitment to attain your Target Zones. Target Zone 1 (ten years from now): _____

What *must* happen in one year for you to be on track to reaching this target?
_____
_____
_____

_____
_____
_____

    Based on the paragraph above, what are the top five things that need to happen in one year for you to reach this target, and why?

1) _____
   Why? _____
_____
_____
_____
_____

2) _____
   Why? _____
_____
_____
_____
_____

3) _____
   Why? _____
_____
_____
_____
_____

4) _____
   Why? _____
_____
_____
_____
_____

5) _____
   Why? _____
_____
_____
_____
_____

Brutally Honest Life Management Journal

As you move down the Brutally Honest Success Pathway and attempt to expand your Brutally Honest Veil of Comfort, you will experience setbacks and failures. In this first year, it is critically important to identify what may stand in your way. These may be real threats or simply self-imposed doubt. Either way, real or imagined, by the initial act of anticipating their occurrence, you are reducing their chances of derailing your quest. You will then have, in advance, a plan to overcome these obstacles, should they occur.

List five obstacles that could impede your attainment of this one-year target.

1) _____
2) _____
3) _____
4) _____
5) _____

Why might these obstacles occur? _____
_____
_____
_____
_____

How could they adversely affect you? _____
_____
_____
_____
_____

Are there things you can do today to minimize the chances of these obstacles occurring, or are they outside of your control? _____
_____
_____
_____
_____

The momentum you create during this first year is crucial. It will add fuel to the process. The right people can add to this momentum and exponentially increase your chances of success. So, too, can the wrong people detract from your chances of success. Choose wisely. Sometimes even the people whom we like to be with are not the right people to help us achieve our Brutally Honest Target Zones.

Who will you reach out to during this first year to help you gain leverage and ensure that your one-year targets are on track? Compare this list to the one created during the five-year Target Zone exercise. Are they the same people? If not, why? Use this comparison as a way of continuing to learn and to grow. In life we will often find that those whom we thought we could count on, simply let us down, while others whom we may never of thought could help us, help us in ways that had previously been unimaginable. The lesson here is to never speak in absolutes. Always leave open additional possibilities and embrace change.

List people who can help you reach this one-year target and state *why* each is important.

Person: _____
Relationship: _____
    Why? _____
_____
_____
_____
_____

Person: _____
Relationship: _____
    Why? _____
_____
_____
_____
_____

Person: _____
Relationship: _____
    Why? _____
_____
_____
_____
_____

Person: _____
Relationship: _____
    Why? _____
_____
_____
_____
_____

Brutally Honest Life Management Journal

Person: _____
Relationship: _____
   Why? _____
_____
_____
_____

   Just as the right people add to your leverage during the first year, so too do the right things. Below, list things that you can utilize to give you added leverage and why they will help you.

Thing: _____
   Why? _____
_____
_____
_____
_____

Thing: _____
   Why? _____
_____
_____
_____
_____

Thing: _____
   Why? _____
_____
_____
_____
_____

Thing: _____
   Why? _____
_____
_____
_____
_____

Thing: _____
   Why? _____

Thing: _____
    Why? _____

Lastly, for this Target Zone, write a one-paragraph Brutally Honest Power Statement indicating why achieving this target is an absolute must.

> *We imitate only what we believe and admire.*
>   —Robert Aris Willmott

Target Zone 2 (ten years from now): _____
    What *must* happen in one year for you to be on track to reaching this target?

Based on the paragraph above, what are the top five things that need to happen

Brutally Honest Life Management Journal

in one year for you to be on track to reaching this target, and why?

1) _____

   Why? _____
_____
_____
_____
_____

2) _____

   Why? _____
_____
_____
_____
_____

3) _____

   Why? _____
_____
_____
_____
_____

4) _____

   Why? _____
_____
_____
_____
_____

5) _____

   Why? _____
_____
_____
_____
_____

   List five obstacles that could impede your attainment of this one-year target.

1)_____
2)_____
3)_____
4)_____

5) _____

    Why might these obstacles occur?

_____
_____
_____
_____

    How could they adversely affect you?

_____
_____
_____
_____

    Are there things you can do today to minimize the chances of these obstacles occurring, or are they outside of your control?

_____
_____
_____
_____

    List people who can help you reach this one-year target and state *why* each is important.

Person: _____
Relationship: _____
    Why? _____
_____
_____
_____

Person: _____
Relationship: _____
    Why? _____
_____
_____
_____

Brutally Honest Life Management Journal

Person: _____
Relationship: _____
   Why? _____
_____
_____
_____
_____
_____

Person: _____
Relationship: _____
   Why? _____
_____
_____
_____
_____
_____

Person: _____
Relationship: _____
   Why? _____
_____
_____
_____
_____

    Just as the right people add to your leverage during the first year, so too do the right things. Below, list things that you can utilize to give you added leverage and why they will help you.

Thing: _____
   Why? _____
_____
_____
_____

Thing: _____
   Why? _____
_____
_____

Thing: _____
    Why? _____
    _____
    _____
    _____

Thing: _____
    Why? _____
    _____
    _____
    _____

Thing: _____
    Why? _____
    _____
    _____
    _____

Thing: _____
    Why? _____
    _____
    _____
    _____

Lastly, for this Target Zone, write a one-paragraph Brutally Honest Power Statement indicating why achieving this target is an absolute must.

_____
_____
_____
_____

Target Zone 3 (ten years from now): _____
    What must happen in one year for you to be on track to reaching this target?

Based on the paragraph above, what are the top five things that need to happen in one year for you to be on track to reaching this target, and why?

1) _____
   Why? _____

2) _____
   Why? _____

3) _____
   Why? _____

4) _____
   Why? _____

5) _____
   Why? _____

List five obstacles that could impede your attainment of this one-year target.

1) _____
2) _____
3) _____
4) _____
5) _____

Why might these obstacles occur?

_____
_____
_____
_____

How could they adversely affect you?

_____
_____
_____
_____

Are there things you can do today to minimize the chances of these obstacles occurring, or are they outside of your control?

_____
_____
_____
_____

List people who can help you reach this one-year target and state *why* each is important.

Person: _____
Relationship: _____
 Why? _____
_____
_____
_____

Person: _____
Relationship: _____
 Why? _____
_____

Person: _____
Relationship: _____
   Why? _____

Person: _____
Relationship: _____
   Why? _____

Person: _____
Relationship: _____
   Why? _____

Just as the right people add to your leverage during the first year, so too do the right things. Below, list things that you can utilize to give you added leverage and why they will help you.

Thing: _____
   Why? _____

Thing: _____
   Why? _____

_____
_____

Thing: _____
    Why? _____
_____
_____
_____

Thing: _____
    Why? _____
_____
_____
_____

Thing: _____
    Why? _____
_____
_____
_____

Thing: _____
    Why? _____
_____
_____
_____

Lastly, for this Target Zone, write a one-paragraph Brutally Honest Power Statement indicating why achieving this target is an absolute must.

_____
_____
_____
_____
_____

Brutally Honest Life Management Journal

> *Victory belongs to the most persevering.*
> —Napoleon Bonaparte

Target Zone 4 (ten years from now): _____

What *must* happen in one year for you to be on track to reaching this target?

_____
_____
_____
_____

Based on the paragraph above, what are the top five things that need to happen in one year for you to be on track to reaching this target, and why?

1) _____
   Why? _____
   _____
   _____
   _____

2) _____
   Why? _____
   _____
   _____
   _____

3) _____
   Why? _____
   _____
   _____
   _____

4) _____
   Why? _____
   _____

_____
_____
_____

5) _____
    Why? _____
_____
_____
_____

    List five obstacles that could impede your attainment of this one-year target.

1) _____
2) _____
3) _____
4) _____
5) _____

Why might these obstacles occur?
_____
_____
_____
_____

How could they adversely affect you? _____
_____
_____
_____
_____

    Are there things you can do today to minimize the chances of these obstacles occurring, or are they outside of your control?
_____
_____
_____

    List people who can help you reach this one-year target and state *why* each is important.

Person: _____
Relationship: _____

Why? _____
_____
_____
_____
_____

Person: _____
Relationship: _____
　Why? _____
_____
_____
_____
_____
_____

Person: _____
Relationship: _____
　Why? _____
_____
_____
_____
_____
_____

Person: _____
Relationship: _____
　Why? _____
_____
_____
_____
_____
_____

Person: _____
Relationship: _____
　Why? _____
_____
_____
_____
_____
_____

　　Just as the right people add to your leverage during the first year, so too do the right things. Below, list things that you can utilize to give you added leverage and why they will help you.

Thing: _____
   Why? _____
   _____
   _____
   _____
   _____

Thing: _____
   Why? _____
   _____
   _____
   _____
   _____

Thing: _____
   Why? _____
   _____
   _____
   _____
   _____

Thing: _____
   Why? _____
   _____
   _____
   _____
   _____

Thing: _____
   Why? _____
   _____
   _____
   _____
   _____

Thing: _____
   Why? _____
   _____
   _____
   _____
   _____

> ### *Jim*
>
> I was eighteen, on my own, and without two dimes to rub together. I lived where I could and relied on the compassion of friends. As I said before, I was just existing each day and partying too much to drown the pain at night. One morning, as I sat up in bed with my head pounding, I said out loud in a sarcastic manner, "It's just another day in paradise." I laughed at the ridiculous notion that this could be paradise, but while I was laughing I realized that my hideous surroundings did not seem so bad.
>
> I allowed my brain to grasp the fact that maybe this was paradise. Maybe just being alive for another day to breathe the air and feel the sunshine was paradise. But even if it was not, it just felt good to say it. At that time I did not know that I was stumbling onto a whole field of study about positive thought and the effect it has on us all. All I knew was that when I said, "It is just another day in paradise," and laughed about it, I felt better. The world looked a good bit more friendly, and the weight I had imposed on myself lifted a bit.
>
> Could it be that each of us has an empowering Brutally Honest Power Statement that could change our attitude in a millisecond if we just believed or even just tried it? The answer is simply yes. Wow! Think of the power of what we just found out. We found out that we can actually control our outlook by our thoughts and physical actions (for example, laughing and smiling). I really want you to think about this in creating your Brutally Honest Power Statement. Make sure it is something that you really can get behind and that has significant meaning in your life. Allow yourself to receive the gift of instant peace of mind any time you want it!

Lastly, for this Target Zone, write a one-paragraph Brutally Honest Power Statement indicating why achieving this target is an absolute must.

_____
_____
_____
_____
_____

Target Zone 5 (ten years from now): _____
What *must* happen in one year for you to be on track to reaching this target?

_____
_____
_____
_____

Based on the paragraph above, what are the top five things that need to happen in one year for you to be on track to reaching this target, and why?

1) _____
   Why? _____
   _____
   _____
   _____

2) _____
   Why? _____
   _____
   _____
   _____

3) _____
   Why? _____
   _____
   _____
   _____

4) _____
   Why? _____
   _____
   _____
   _____

5) _____

Why? _____
_____
_____
_____
_____

> *Patience is power; with time and patience the mulberry leaf becomes silk.*
> —Chinese Proverb

List five obstacles that could impede your attainment of this one-year target.

1) _____
2) _____
3) _____
4) _____
5) _____

Why might these obstacles occur?
_____
_____
_____
_____

How could they adversely affect you?
_____
_____
_____
_____

Are there things you can do today to minimize the chances of these obstacles occurring, or are they outside of your control? _____
_____
_____
_____
_____

List people who can help you reach this one-year target and state *why* each is important.

Person: _____
Relationship: _____

Why? _____
_____
_____
_____
_____

Person: _____
Relationship: _____
Why? _____
_____
_____
_____
_____

Person: _____
Relationship: _____
Why? _____
_____
_____
_____
_____

Person: _____
Relationship: _____
Why? _____
_____
_____
_____
_____

Person: _____
Relationship: _____
Why? _____
_____
_____
_____
_____

Just as the right people add to your leverage during the first year, so too do the right things. Below, list things that you can utilize to give you added leverage and why they will help you.

Brutally Honest Life Management Journal

Thing: _____
    Why? _____
_____
_____
_____
_____

Thing: _____
    Why? _____
_____
_____
_____
_____

Thing: _____
    Why? _____
_____
_____
_____
_____

Thing: _____
    Why? _____
_____
_____
_____
_____

Thing: _____
    Why? _____
_____
_____
_____
_____

Thing: _____
    Why? _____
_____
_____
_____
_____

Lastly, for this Target Zone, write a one-paragraph Brutally Honest Power Statement indicating why achieving this target is an absolute must.

_____
_____
_____
_____

You did it! You have now assessed your one-year targets and put together a detailed plan to help move you closer to your Brutally Honest Target Zones. Seeing the bull's-eye in front of you, you have picked up the bow, gripped it firmly, aimed at the targets, gently pulled back on the string, and are ready to release.

> *An ungrateful man is like a hog under a tree eating acorns, but never looking up to see where they come from.*
> —Timothy Dexter

Stage III: Quest for Utopia

Having created your Brutally Honest Life Plan, the journey to Utopia continues. The journey is an ongoing work-in-progress to not only reach the goals set in one's Brutally Honest Life Plan, but to learn the critical skills of self-evaluation as the journey unfolds. Most programs teach setting goals and how to achieve them. While this is admirable, the reality is that no plan can be left unchecked. In the process of transcending through your Brutally Honest Life Plan, you must continue to define, evaluate, re-evaluate, and improve.

You will learn the skill of adaptation and how to develop the mindset to react quickly to life's curveballs. You will be able and ready to spread the word to others. One of the most rewarding things that we can do is to mentor others and make a real difference in others' lives. Frankly, that is the reason Brutally Honest exists.

> *Utopia is the never-ending pursuit of excellence measured by the satisfaction of living life to the fullest. True Utopia incorporates a life in which you are the mentor and you are able to help others.*
>
> Gregory LaMonaca

Congratulations! You have now done more than 95 percent of Americans. You have taken—and are continuing to take—steps toward attaining your compelling future by way of achieving your Brutally Honest Target Zones. We need to carry this momentum forward. You know that the mapping process involves more than simply writing your ten-, five-, and one-year goals. If we currently live in Florida and want to map out our trip to California, would we start our map from Texas? Of course not! We would start from our current location, Florida, wouldn't we?

Similarly, through analyzing your past and present, you have created a clearly defined starting point. To continue our metaphor, you went beyond simply saying, "I am starting somewhere on the East Coast," and identified Palm Beach.

If you don't know where you are going you will probably end up somewhere else.
—Laurence Johnson Peter

In addition to creating a clearly defined starting point, by examining your ten-year, five-year, and one-year Brutally Honest Target Zones, you have also clearly defined your destination. When you started this journal, you probably would have said, "I want to go to California"—an admirable goal, but one lacking in specificity. With this sort of goal, as for most Americans who wish for things (money, big homes, fancy cars), the goal would remain just a dream. You, on the other hand, have created crystal clear, vivid goals. Your destination is defined as "sunny Anaheim, California," which is further refined to "Disneyland," and further broken down to waiting in line to ride Space Mountain and then plunging down the ride's first enormous descent!

Through carefully breaking down and refining your Brutally Honest Target Zones from your Ten-Year Day-in-the-Life Statement to your ten-year Target Zones, then to your five-year and one-year Target Zones, your vision has been made crystal clear. You can feel yourself holding on to the safety bars on the Space Mountain ride as you fly through the dark. You can hear the sounds of the rumbling ride and the screams of fellow riders. You can see the flashing lights, the darkness, the dips, bends, and twists in front of you. You can taste the atmosphere and smell the aroma that surrounds you.

With this in mind, you have now created the map. You have packed your bags, arrived at the airport, and need only to board the plane as you prepare to jet off to sunny California.

"The Trip" A Note from Your Soul

I am truly very proud of you! We have connected in a way that few can. As your soul, I was once detached and uninvolved. You didn't want to know me, feel me, sense me, or embrace me. But now we are truly one. Thank you for your courage and commitment to do this. We are now intimately connected in a way that cannot be severed. You have taken an introspective journey from your past to the present. Through this process, our two worlds came together as one.

As you move forward, you must utilize all of the tools we have gathered throughout our journey. You too can see the path. Now is the time to move into the future.

> *Frequently, the difference between success and failure is the resolve to stick to your plan long enough to win.*
> —David Cottrell

Enter the Zone

You're now committed, dedicated, and prepared to weather the storm. It's time to take action. As you do, your Brutally Honest Toolbox will accompany you, providing the tools you'll need as you traverse the Brutally Honest Success Pathway. The tools you carry will be unique to you. You have already picked up many tools thus far and will continue to add to your box as your journey unfolds.

As you venture forward, you want to ensure your Brutally Honest Toolbox is packed to capacity. What tools are inside? Why are they important? Your tools will always be with you. Anytime you encounter a roadblock you will simply reach into your toolbox and take out the appropriate tool to get you over or through the roadblock. Through your conditioning, you have created adaptation skills. As with the old, rusty tools that accumulate in our real toolboxes, it's time to replace the old with the new. Often we develop a comfort level with the old and are reluctant to let go of the past and leap out into the future by trying new tools. More often than not, once we take the leap and try something new, at the same time letting go of the past, we are positively surprised over what we find.

Brutally Honest tools are *not* your family, your friends, or the things listed in your one-year Target Zone exercise. You're in the big leagues now, the advanced class. As you now know, you are in the top 5 percent simply because you took the time to create this journal. While that is outstanding, we are now going to forge even further into the depths of your Brutally Honest Empowerment Zone. What is this zone? It's a place of absolute serenity, a place where your troubles are nonexistent and all the cares and troubles in your life are temporarily suspended. Have you ever been to such a place? We have all had times when we were exhilarated and passionate—in a state of absolute bliss—when we felt invincible, unstoppable, and determined and everything just seemed to go right. These times, while powerful, are few and far between. Because of your ongoing focus, determination, and commitment to excellence, you are ready to seek out these zones. The result will be more times of bliss and serenity.

When you are in the Brutally Honest Empowerment Zone, you are unstoppable. You feel a sense of controlled invincibility. Here, in this state, you are most likely to accomplish what you seek. Your reticular activating system is on high alert. Since our desired outcome is the attainment of our Brutally Honest Target Zones, it follows that we will increase our likelihood of attaining these targets if we can spend more time in the Zone. With each tool you add to your Brutally Honest Toolbox, you will increase the likelihood of arriving at this magical place.

A tool is a state of mind, and a state of mind is a place that your mind occupies at any given time. There are of course positive states and negative states. Clearly our mission is to seek out these positive states and avoid the negative ones.

Examples of positive states or emotions:
- Elation
- Happiness
- Joy
- Bliss
- Motivation
- Excitement
- Empathy
- Honesty
- Integrity

Examples of negative states or emotions:
- Depression
- Anger
- Disappointment
- Frustration
- Worry
- Fear
- Anxiety
- Jealousy

Of course, you have experienced the majority of these emotions listed above at different times in your life. Many of these states are listed in your assessment of your past and present. What makes us dwell on one thing over another? While many factors contribute to this, the most central is focus. You have the power within you to instantly change your state. As simple as this may sound, it is one of the most powerful tools you will carry with you.

Focus is a major component of all highly successful individuals. A laser-guided focus helps us prioritize and create bonded links between our Brutally Honest Target Zones and our reticular activating system. Our world, with all of its many distractions, will constantly attempt to derail your focus. As a result, your positive focus is a significant tool to keep in your Brutally Honest Toolbox.

Brutally Honest Life Management Journal

How *you* define and prioritize your focus will make a difference. Give it a powerful name, something that will link its power to your reticular activating system. For example, Greg coined the phrase *laser-beam focus*. As Jim (with his master's degree in engineering) has pointed out on many occasions, the word *laser beam* is probably better left to old science fiction movies and the proper usage of the term would simply be *laser focus*. (There is a price to be paid for having an engineer as a partner.) The bottom line is it doesn't matter what you call

> *The most powerful fighter is an ordinary man with laser precision focus.*
> —Bruce Lee

it or how "out there" your name is. It is for you and only you. Make it funny, silly, powerful, dynamic, or all of the above.

My name for my tool of focus is_____.

My _____focus is important for my success because:
_____
_____
_____
_____.

As significant as focus is to your success, so too is your state—not where you reside physically but where your mind resides at any given time. The state *you* choose to be in will determine how you feel. If it is truly this simple, why then do we sometimes choose to be in a negative state? The answer lies not in the choice of *whether* to be in a positive or negative state, but instead in *who* chooses. As we have learned throughout our journey together, there will be an incredible number of outside influences that will fight to determine how you feel. By arriving at Soul's Core, you created Brutally Honest Filters that run in the background of your mind, filtering out the outside influences that are not consistent with your Brutally Honest Target Zones.

When you watch a horror film such as *Friday the 13th* the producers do everything possible to create the emotion of fear. In a movie like *Brian's Song*, emotions such as empathy and sadness run wild. In these situations, we *choose* to subject ourselves to these emotional states.

What happens, however, when you are confronted with all of the stress that the world brings each day? During the course of a single day, you are pounded by thousands of competing emotions, some good and some bad. How you react to these emotions determines how you feel. Creating defense filters will allow only those emotions that *you* choose to let into your mind.

In the following exercise, choose a representative day from the previous week and one weekend day. Describe in vivid detail your day from the time you awoke until the time you went to bed, being sure to list *every* emotion that you encountered, positive or negative. It should be a Brutally Honest Emotional Volcano, erupting with honesty, clarity, and forthrightness.

Weekday Brutally Honest Emotional Volcano

Now do the same thing for a representative weekend day.

Weekend Brutally Honest Emotional Volcano

Brutally Honest Life Management Journal

How do you feel? Were you truly Brutally Honest? Now go back and underline every emotion that you encountered during the two days. You will find as you do this that you will recall additional emotions from both your weekday and weekend Emotional Volcanoes. List these additional emotions below. Remember that you want an all-inclusive list. Even if the emotion was momentary, list it.

Additional emotions from Weekday Brutally Honest Emotional Volcano:

_____
_____
_____
_____

Additional emotions from Weekend Brutally Honest Emotional Volcano:

_____
_____
_____
_____
_____
_____
_____

Negative Emotions

Now, by combining all of the emotions you came up with from both the weekday and weekend lists above, separate all of these emotions into two categories: negative and positive.

From your Emotional Volcanos, list all of the negative emotions below:

_____
_____
_____
_____

Jim

Let me ask you a question: do you control your emotions or do your emotions control you? Have you ever really asked yourself this question, or is it to scary to think about? I ask this jokingly because if you have gotten this far you already know how to control your emotions and use your emotions in a very positive way.

Every day I meet with my staff at Ultimate Image Salon and Spa to coach and mentor them. Our staff ranges in age from eighteen to fifty-plus. In our coaching sessions we go over a number of goals and ways that they can increase their earnings, but much more important, we talk about life. We discuss their emotional states and how they affect their business. Brutally Honest is the method I use to coach and mentor my staff, and they have done phenomenally. Our business has more than doubled in six years, and everyone grows year after year.

Emotions are always a topic for discussion, but we do not dwell on the negative. Instead we figure out ways to use emotions—both negative and positive—as motivating tools. I know this makes the staff feel empowered. It gives control of their lives back to them. Learning how to use positive and negative emotions to your benefit is one of the greatest tools you will ever put in your Brutally Honest Toolbox. Please write down what I am about to tell you and keep it somewhere where you will see it first thing in the morning and right before you go to sleep. Are you ready, with your pen in hand? Here it is: *You and you alone control your mind. Your mind does not control you.*

Brutally Honest Life Management Journal

_____
_____
_____
_____
_____
_____
_____

Out of the list above, list below the five most negative emotions that affect you during the course of a week, with number one being the most negative and number five being the least negative. List only those emotions that are the most repetitive.

1) _____
2) _____
3) _____
4) _____
5) _____

Patterns appear in all areas of our lives. Understanding why and how we do things provides the cornerstone of our success. Do you wake up at the same time each day, take a shower, brush your teeth, get dressed, put the pot of coffee on, walk out and get the paper, come inside, turn on the morning news, read the paper as you eat your breakfast and drink your coffee, and then head out to work, driving the same exact route as you have always done before? Patterns are everywhere. Understanding your own patterns, both good and bad, and how they affect you, will help you continue to move forward toward your Brutally Honest Target Zones.

> *Learning gives us a fuller conviction of the imperfections of our nature; which one would think, might dispose us to modesty: for the more a man knows, the more he discovers his ignorance.*
> —Jeremy Collier

Looking at the top five above, determine if there are any patterns as to when, why, where, and with whom they tend to appear. Write the patterns below:

_____
_____
_____
_____
_____
_____

Our senses are central to anchoring an emotion to an event. What we see, hear, smell, touch, and taste create anchors in our reticular activating system. An anchor is any representation (internally or externally generated) that triggers another representation or series of representations. Whenever any portion of a particular experience is reintroduced, other portions of that experience will be reproduced to some degree. We call these representations, Brutally Honest Links.

When you review your top five negative emotions and think of them collectively, determine how each of your senses associates with them. For example, you may be fearful when you are in dark (sight) places or when you hear loud sounds. The same stimuli (darkness) in another person might create a sense of serenity and security as they associate darkness with sleeping.

Sight:

_____
_____
_____
_____

Hearing:

_____
_____
_____
_____

Smell:

_____
_____
_____
_____

Touch:

_____
_____
_____
_____

Taste:
_____
_____
_____
_____

Did you find certain patterns that brought about your negative emotions? Did you determine that they occur when certain stimuli are present, which then get anchored to your reticular activating system when you interpret these stimuli through your senses?

By reviewing all of the above, what changes can you make immediately to eliminate or modify your negative emotions?
_____
_____
_____
_____

Why *must* you eliminate these negative emotions in order to achieve your Brutally Honest Target Zones?
_____
_____
_____
_____

Let's now move on to the emotions that will catapult you to the next level and truly empower you. Let's look at your positive emotions.

Positive Emotions

From your Emotional Volcanos, list all of the positive emotions below:
_____
_____
_____
_____
_____

    Out of the list above, take out the five most positive emotions that affect you during the course of a week, with number one being the most positive and number five being the least positive. List only those emotions that are the most repetitive.

1) _____
2) _____
3) _____
4) _____
5) _____

    Each of these positive emotions is a tool to add to your Brutally Honest Toolbox. Just like you came up with your own unique name for your focus, so too will you need to come up with unique and powerful names for each of your top five emotions, in addition to determining why each emotional tool is important to your success.

Positive Emotion 1: _____
My unique name for this positive emotional tool is_____.
    My _____(write unique name) is essential for my success because:
_____
_____
_____
_____

Positive Emotion 2: _____
My unique name for this positive emotional tool is_____.
    My _____(write unique name) is essential for my success because:
_____
_____
_____
_____

Positive Emotion 3: _____

My unique name for this positive emotional tool is_____.

    My _____ (write unique name) is essential for my success because:

_____
_____
_____
_____
_____

Positive Emotion 4: _____

My unique name for this positive emotional tool is_____.

    My _____ (write unique name) is essential for my success because:

_____
_____
_____
_____
_____

Positive Emotion 5: _____

My unique name for this positive emotional tool is_____.

    My _____ (write unique name) is essential for my success because:

_____
_____
_____
_____
_____

> *Money is not required to buy one necessity of the soul.*
> —Henry David Thoreau

    In order to achieve our Brutally Honest Target Zones, we *must* determine what patterns exist in our lives that bring about our positive emotions. If successful, we can replicate these patterns to bring about similar emotions.

    Looking at the top five above, determine if there are any patterns as to when, why, where, and with whom they tend to appear. Write the patterns below:

_____
_____

As we learned, our senses are central to anchoring an emotion to an event. What we see, hear, smell, touch, and taste during the time we encounter a positive emotion creates associations in our reticular activating system.

For example, this journal is the sum total of hundreds of hours of preparation and more than eighteen years of research. Greg often found it difficult determining when he could write. He attempted many times to do so during the week at home, only to find himself uninspired, yielding minimal, if any, results. The pressures of daily life squashed his creativity and desire to write. Then, one weekend at his mountain home, Greg awoke at 5:00 AM, well before his wife and children, went downstairs, put a pot of coffee on, and took his dog Tasha outside for a walk behind the house. The sun had just recently risen, its brilliant radiance shining throughout the woodland pasture (sight). The smell of the morning dew, trees, and nature filled every ounce of Greg's being (smell). As he and Tasha navigated the uneven path below their feet, Greg could feel nature's magic below him (touch).

After their walk, Greg and Tasha went back inside where the aroma of coffee filled the house (smell). He poured a cup and indulged in his morning elixir (taste). Once done, he went to the computer and opened up Apple's iTunes Jukebox software which housed a few of his children's albums, which had been saved there to transfer to and use with their iPods. One album was the soundtrack to the movie *Brother Bear*. He put his headphones on, blasted (hearing) the soundtrack, and began writing this journal. This sequence of events was replicated over and over each time he was at the mountains, each time creating an amazing environment that allowed him to have absolute serenity and peak creativity.

As soon as Greg hears any song from that soundtrack, his reticular activating system immediately brings him back to that same place of serenity. When he explained this to Jim during one of their weekly Brutally Honest meetings, he suggested that Greg try to replicate this environment at his home office. Greg was initially resistant, indicating that the environment that he had created at the mountains was special and unique and that he would not want the feeling of serenity to be replaced by the negative pressures of daily life.

The following week, while at his home, Greg awoke at 5:00 AM again, while the children and his wife slept. He went downstairs, put a pot of coffee on, opened the back door, and let Tasha run out into the gated yard behind the house. Like it had at his mountain home, the sun had just recently risen with similar brilliance and radiance, shining throughout the yard and reflecting off the pool in many directions (sight). The smell of the morning air, while different from that up in the mountains, was equally addictive (smell). He leaned over the deck and felt the rough texture of its railing in his hand (touch).

He and Tasha went back inside where the same aroma of coffee that had filled his mountain home again filled the air (smell). He poured a cup of the same elixir (taste), putting his senses on red alert. Once done, he went to his home office and booted up the computer. He opened the same iTunes Jukebox program, cranked up *Brother Bear*, and began to write. What he had thought could not happen, happened. By recreating the same stimuli and sequence of events from the mountains, Greg was able to regain the same positive state. Through the stimulation of his senses and the replication of things that had affected him at the mountains, he was able to recapture the same serenity. The positive experience that he'd had at the mountains was now anchored in his reticular activating system. Through this process, a Brutally Honest Link was created between the positive experiences he'd had at the mountains to the newfound similar positive experience at his home office. Was this just a mere coincidence? Well, more than a year passed between Greg's beginning work on this and moving into the editing stage. And Greg still found himself in his home office, early in the morning, after letting Tasha outside, with the *Brother Bear* soundtrack cranked up. The same creativity, passion, and emotions that he had felt that first time he'd played the music at the Pocono's was still being recreated.

The goal, therefore, is to create as many positive links as possible. These links collectively form an unbreakable chain that can be recalled at will to instantly bring you back into the same positive state.

> *Steady, patient, persevering thinking will generally surmount every obstacle in search after truth.*
> —Nathaniel Emmons

When you review your top five positive emotions, and think of them collectively, determine how each of your sense's associates with them.

Sight:
_____
_____
_____
_____
_____
_____

Hearing:
_____
_____
_____
_____
_____
_____

Smell:
_____
_____
_____
_____
_____
_____

Touch:
_____
_____
_____

Taste:
_____
_____
_____

Brutally Honest Life Management Journal

> ### Jim
>
> I remember sitting with my mom in her hospital room, listening to music together. I held her frail hand and watched her breathe. At that point breathing was not an easy thing for her. The song we would listen to over and over was one from the *Rocky* soundtrack, entitled "Mickey." The song was an instrumental, which changed themes many times throughout. When the song ended, I would rewind the cassette and begin it again. Many nights the nurses let me stay much later than they should have. I would sit and talk to her and tell her about my day and how much I loved her. I don't know how much she understood, but every once in a while she would gently squeeze my hand.
>
> Even today, every time I hear that song I am taken back to that hospital room. Every time I smell a hospital I am taken back to those last days spending time with the most influential person in my life. Every time I see someone struggling to hang on I am taken back to the memory of Mom. I hope by now you really understand the absolute power of your senses and how they make you feel. You can use this power to keep your self in peak motivation. You can also use this knowledge to avoid sensory input that takes you down a dark path. Sometimes, when I just want to cry, I will put on that song and instantly tears come to my eyes. I can see why you might wonder why I would purposely do this to myself. The reality is that the song is a link to her and my tears are in tribute to a life of love. Please use the power of your senses wisely.

Can you see how powerful your senses are in creating your Brutally Honest Links as we continue to move forward?

rewrite your ten-year Brutally Honest Target Zones below. (Note: By this point you should have them memorized.)

Target Zone 1: _____
Target Zone 2: _____
Target Zone 3: _____
Target Zone 4: _____
Target Zone 5: _____

If, through the utilization of our senses, we take the same sequence of events that gave rise to our positive emotions and intertwine them with our Brutally Honest Target Zones, doesn't it make sense that we could increase our chances of success?

Below, describe in vivid detail how your senses can be used to assist in reaching each of the Target Zones:

Target Zone 1: _____

Sight:

_____
_____
_____
_____
_____

Hearing:

_____
_____
_____
_____
_____

Smell:

_____
_____
_____
_____
_____

Touch:

_____
_____
_____
_____
_____

Taste:

_____
_____
_____
_____
_____

Target Zone 2: _____
Sight:

Hearing:

Smell:

Touch:

Taste:

> *The surest way not to fail is to determine to succeed.*
> —Richard Brinsley Sheridan

Target Zone 3: _____

Sight:

Hearing:

Smell:

Touch:

Taste:

Brutally Honest Life Management Journal

Target Zone 4: _____
Sight:
_____
_____
_____
_____

Hearing:
_____
_____
_____
_____

Smell:
_____
_____
_____
_____

Touch:
_____
_____
_____
_____

Taste:
_____
_____
_____
_____

Target Zone 5: _____
Sight:
_____

Hearing:

Smell:

Touch:

Taste:

Go forward now with the added confidence of knowing *you* are equipped with the ability to determine what emotions you experience and when and how you choose to encounter them.

> *Our real blessings often appear to us in the shape of pains, losses, and disappointments; but let us have patience, and we soon shall see them in their proper figures.*
> —Joseph Addison

Substituting Emotions

We have learned how our senses play an important role in how we interpret various stimuli and the meaning we give them. Advertisers are masters of this. Every advertisement that we see, whether a billboard, television commercial, or magazine advertisement, is the product of hundreds of hours of research on human behavior. Through everything from the sight, sound, feel, and arrangement of the ads to the people who appear in the ads, companies painstakingly attempt to get you to buy their products, use their services, or do any number of things. Companies pay marketing firms hundreds of thousands of dollars to do one simple thing: get you to do something *they* want you to do.

On November 1, 2008, we were just days away from having a new president of the United States. You couldn't turn on the radio, read a paper, watch television, or drive around the neighborhood without being infiltrated with each party's advertisements, all attempting to convince you of who to vote for. Some ads were designed to evoke passion, energy, empathy, or loyalty. Other ads were focused on what the other candidate had done wrong or would do wrong. In the end, it was all highly thought-out marketing designed to control our minds.

What you have learned, however, is that you can filter out these things, as well as other negative societal pressures, and instead allow in only those things that positively affect you by consciously predetermining what to let in. This conditioning takes place in your reticular activating system, which becomes a twenty-four-hour radar system, only letting in those things that you have told it to. This assumes however that you have programmed your reticular activating system to look for these positive things and that the things programmed are in fact positive.

What happens, however, when our reticular activating system gets conflicting signals and the same stimulus causes both positive and negative emotions at the same time? Let's take a look at the story of Tony and Sarah.

It is not a problem when internal representations are in harmony. Perhaps Sarah and Tony both share a passion for yellow roses. Every time they see them, they both marvel over the beauty of these most precious gifts from God. As Sarah sees yellow roses, her mind links all of the rose's traits with linked positive associations.

The problem occurs where there are conflicting internal representations. If Sarah loves yellow roses and Tony hates them, there will exist the possibility of future negative associations in Sarah's mind when she sees yellow roses. If the internal battle is significant enough, it could cause guilt in Sarah's mind.

Brutally Honest Life Management Journal

This occurs within each of us every second of our lives. Images and associations are constantly being stored based upon our perceptions and subsequent internalization in our minds. Do we link positive or negative traits to an item? The answer will determine how we later perceive the same, or similar, thing in the future when confronted with it again. What meaning we link with the perception will determine how we later feel about it.

For example, while on vacation one summer with her parents when she was young, Sarah visited Longwood Gardens, a botanical wonderland of trees, plants, flowers, and every conceivable arrangement of Earth's beauty, located in suburban Philadelphia. While there, she came upon an amazing assortment of roses, mostly yellow ones, which left a positive, indelible mark in her mind. Each time she saw a yellow rose growing up, it immediately brought her mind back to the beautiful assortment she saw that wonderfully warm July day. Her mind was programmed to associate yellow roses with pleasure.

Growing up, Tony had a favorite uncle, Vito. Uncle Vito would visit often and would always have a handful of change and toys to give Tony. Uncle Vito was the person who taught Tony how to fish and was there when he caught his first fish. Amazingly however, in the picture Uncle Vito took of Tony holding up his first fish, all you could see in the photo was Little Tony, all of seven years old, with the biggest smile and his outstretched arm holding his first catch. The fish, however, was covered by Uncle Vito's thumb, which apparently had been partially covering the lens. The result was a complete picture memorializing this one-time event, without the most prized part—the fish. When Tony was eleven, Uncle Vito passed away. Tony was devastated when he heard the news from his father. He wept by himself in his room as he recalled all of the great things Vito and he had done together. That week, he attended the funeral. As he watched his father eulogize Uncle Vito, he noticed that on both sides of the casket there were assortments of yellow roses; and his mind linked yellow roses with sadness and loss. Thereafter, whenever Tony would see yellow roses, a feeling of sadness would come over him, without his knowing why.

Your RAS is a powerful tool and one that can shape the course of your destiny. This point is further demonstrated with a story from Jim's youth:

For as long as I could remember, I had loved the beach. Everything about it brought warm and wonderful feelings to me. Just looking at the waves breaking made my heart sing. One of the special treasures in my childhood was walking hand in hand with my mother collecting shells. On vacations, she and I would wake up before my father and sisters awoke and sneak out of the hotel room into a world of beauty and wonderment. It cost us nothing but a little sleep to walk together and explore God's gifts to us. Mom was so special to me, and I remember thinking that if I ever lost her, life would not be the same. The irony was that a few short years later the worst would happen.

Mom died after a six-month battle with what the doctors called galloping cancer, and my life changed forever. Watching her die was the hardest thing that I have ever done. I remember clearly my mother's father saying to me through tearful eyes, "Jimmy, a parent should never outlive their child." I never saw my grandpa cry until the day we buried my mom. I did not fully understand the magnitude of his statement until I became the proud parent of two wonderful little girls, and now I know what Grandpa Meyers meant.

For years I was still drawn to the beach, but it was with mixed and painful emotions. There was a time when I would walk the shoreline taking in the magnificent ocean and then a minute later cry like a small child when I thought of Mom's warm touch and loving look. Even the feeling of warm sand between my toes brought back the memory of her presence but at the same time felt wonderful in the moment.

It took many years and countless pages of journaling to get back my carefree love of the beach. It was only when I took the time to analyze my emotions and what they meant to my reticular activating system that I began to put into place what had happened and truly deal with it.

Unfortunately, most people do not know where to begin; they only know that they have conflicting feelings about an event or a place of a certain time. Only through careful and thoughtful analysis can they set themselves free from the pain and begin to take back their lives.

For now it is sufficient to simply begin to understand the concept of your reticular activating system and to realize that there is a governing force working 24/7 to trigger emotions based on touch, smell, taste, sound, and sight.

> *Life is thick sown with thorns, and I know no other remedy than to pass quickly through them. The longer we dwell on our misfortunes, the greater is their power to harm us.*
> —Francois Marie de Voltaire

Negative associations are not always bad. For example, we all know not to touch thorns or hot stoves because when we were young, we touched them and experienced pain. At that time, we linked these experiences with that pain, and each successive time we touched one of these things, we reinforced the association. Think of it as a layer of cement being placed over the association each time it occurred. Trying to break the association and replace it with something positive becomes increasingly difficult with each layer of cement that is added. To break the association, we must create an association made of dynamite that can destroy the many layers of cement. Once the negative association is destroyed, we can then replace it with a new, positive association so that future occurrences will be linked to this positive thing.

In the above example of Tony and Sarah, if Tony gradually shared his dislike of yellow roses with Sarah, she would begin to have conflicting internal representations of yellow roses, which could cause her to react both positively and negatively at the same time. How we resolve these many daily conflicts will determine how we feel at any given time. These internal conflicts are happening all throughout the day and night with these wars being waged in our subconscious as well as our conscious minds.

The secret is to try to shift the balance strongly to the conscious side so that *we* can control how we react. Taking it a step further, how powerful would it be if we could knowingly squash our negative states, each time they arose, with more powerful, positive states. The reason we get depressed, angry, disappointed, or any of the other negative states we habitually go through, is because at those moments, we empower the negative emotions to a degree that overshadows any of our positive states. In the battle between our positive and negative states, we build up and strengthen the negative emotions to the level of a heavyweight prizefighter. In a seesaw effect, as the negative emotions are strengthened, the corresponding positive emotions are weakened, hence making them the equivalent of a rookie, lightweight fighter. It follows therefore that when the two fighters step into the ring, the negative emotion quickly knocks out the positive one, leaving only the negative emotion to survive and control us.

Throughout the journey we have undertaken together, you have been slowly and consistently tipping the seesaw toward the positive emotion/state side. You have done this by consciously recognizing what makes you encounter positive states as well as negative ones.

We can therefore increase the likelihood of our attaining our Brutally Honest Target Zones by spending more time in positive states. Remember the examples that were given of both negative and positive states. I have rewritten them below:

Examples of positive states or emotions:
- Elation
- Happiness
- Joy
- Bliss
- Motivation
- Excitement
- Empathy
- Honesty
- Integrity

Examples of negative states or emotions:
- Depression
- Anger
- Disappointment
- Frustration
- Worry
- Fear
- Anxiety
- Jealousy

Now it's your turn. In the spaces below, Write your five most frequently experienced negative states, with one representing the least negative state and five representing the most negative state.

Negative States
1) _____
2) _____
3) _____
4) _____
5) _____

Next, in the spaces below, rewrite your five most frequently experienced positive states with one representing the least positive state and five representing the most positive state.

Positive States
1) _____
2) _____
3) _____
4) _____
5) _____

As written above, you can see how there is a fairly even balance between the positive and negative states in that there are five of each and the lists are written in the same size. In theory, if your worst negative state (number five) was matched against *any* of your five positive states, your negative state would win. The power we attributed to each would become the rulebook that your mind used. Now, however, what you will do is begin the process of tipping the seesaw in the direction of the positive states and reprogramming your internal representations. If successful, when your brain is later confronted with one from each list, it will choose the positive one.

(Disempowering your negative emotions/states)

Rewrite all of your five negative states from above on the small lines below.

Negative States
1. _____
2. _____
3. _____
4. _____
5. _____

Was it hard to do? It should have been. Next, rewrite them again in the lines below without writing the numbers. It doesn't matter how small the lines are; make sure you fully rewrite each one.

_____
_____
_____
_____
_____

Now, write zero (0) to the left of each one.

Next, in the bold lines below, rewrite the top five positive states you identified. Write them as large as you can while keeping each on one line.

_____

_____

_____

_____

_____

Now, write a large number five (5) next to each of your positive states. Congratulations! Through this simple exercise, you have begun to reprogram your mind (at least on paper) to overpower future negative emotions with the positive ones. Based upon your newly revised rating scale, all of your negative emotions (now collectively ranked at zero) will be overpowered internally by any of your positive emotions (all now ranked at five).

Like anything else, this may not immediately work every time. It will take conditioning. Like the cement that grew thicker with the negative emotions, each time you consciously focus on this, it will begin to place successive layers of cement, solidifying the positive state.

From this point on you will be consciously aware of what triggers your negative emotions so that you can avoid these triggers. If confronted with a negative emotion, you will immediately substitute any of your positive emotions and consciously, vividly see the positive emotion in your mind destroying the much weaker, negative emotion. You have also programmed your mind to fight any of the negative emotions that may get through your first conscious level and will be handled in your reticular activating system by way of the conditioning you just went through in the last exercise.

As you traverse down your Brutally Honest Success Pathways, the state that you're in at any given time is perhaps the single best determining factor of how quickly and how successfully you will achieve your Brutally Honest Target Zones.

> *Education begins the gentleman, but reading, good company, and reflection must finish him.*
> —John Locke

Your Brutally Honest Power Link

We have learned about the power of positive and negative states, the association between our senses and our emotions, and the concept of anchoring. Next, utilizing these newfound Brutally Honest tools, you will create a symbol for each of your top five Brutally Honest Target Zones.

You know the routine by now. The first step is to rewrite your top five Brutally Honest Target Zones below. Can you do so from memory?

Target Zone 1: _____
Target Zone 2: _____
Target Zone 3: _____
Target Zone 4: _____
Target Zone 5: _____

Now you will create a Brutally Honest Power Link for each one. What is a Power Link? A Power Link is an association that you create which, when recalled, will instantaneously bring you back to a pre-determined state. Of course, all of your Brutally Honest Power Links should be positive. It is a representation measured on a scale from one to ten—one being the lowest and ten being the highest. Get the idea? It's much like a hyperlink to an online website. What happens when you click on a link? It brings you instantaneously to another separate site on the Internet. Of course, whether you are using a telephone line, DSL, or cable will make the difference in how fast you arrive at the other site. Similarly, the Power Links you create can be supercharged based on the effort you put in.

You will now embark on creating individual Power Links for each of your Brutally Honest Target Zones. For this exercise, find a place where you will not be disturbed, where you can let your creative juices flow.

Step One:

For each Target Zone, answer the first sentence with a dynamic, energizing statement as to why you *will* achieve the target. Be creative, using silly words if necessary. For example, you might write, "I will achieve my Target Zone because I am an invincible power broker who commands the respect of my peers and the admiration of my family and who has an unyielding passion and a commitment to excellence."

Step Two:

Close your eyes and create a mental vision of what it will look like when you achieve this Brutally Honest Target Zone. Not just any vision, but a very clear color picture of you living in the moment. Much like when you were developing your Ten-Year Day-in-the-Life Statement, you *must* see yourself having already achieved the target. This step is critical in that the image you create will be what your mind will set out to achieve. As such, as you create your vision, be specific, detailed, and deliberate. For each of us, our targets will be different, but let's look at some examples.

Family and Friends

Who is in your family? Are you married, or do you have a significant other? If so, describe this person in vivid detail. What are their values, wants, and desires? Do they empower you and support your vision? Do you have children? If so, how many? How old are they? What are their activities and hobbies? What are your relationships with your family members like? What types of things do you do with your family? Who are your friends? Who is your best friend? What types of things do you and your friends do together?

Finances

What is your net worth? What does your net worth consist of? How much cash flow do you have? Does it consist of earned income (you work for money), or is it primarily passive income (your money works for you)? Are you the primary breadwinner? Is someone else contributing? What kind of car(s) do you drive? How do you dress and carry yourself?

> *When wealth is lost, nothing is lost; when health is lost, something is lost; when character is lost, all is lost.*
>
> —German Proverb

Living Arrangements

Where are you living? What type of home do you live in? Is it located in the city or on a hundred-acre ranch? How many bedrooms are there? Do you have a pool? Is there a lake, oceanfront, or bay nearby? Do you have a gym or theater room? Does your home have a view? Is it secluded? Does it have gardens or a private entrance? What type of furnishings does it have? Does it contain art or other collectibles? Let your mind begin from when you wake up in your ideal bed in your ideal bedroom. Get out of bed and take a mental walk throughout this ideal home from top to bottom, inside and out. As you do so, describe what you see. You may have multiple homes. Describe them all.

Career

What is your ideal career? Are you working for someone else or for yourself? Describe exactly what you do during your workday. Are you doing something that is consistent with your passion or are you fulfilling someone else's agenda? Where is your work? Is it in a corporate setting, a small office, your home, or outdoors? Are you helping others through your work? Who are you working with or for? Is it a fun environment? Do you have a boss, or are you your own boss? Do your superiors empower you to be your best? Do they want the best for you, or are they only concerned about their agenda? Do they yell at you when you make mistakes, or do they work with you to move past them?

Empowerment

Are you living out your true destiny? Are you an author writing books on your topics of interest? Are you a volunteer at your children's school? Do you lecture to others on topics that you specialize in? Are you pursuing additional schooling? Are you engaging in therapy to overcome past hurt or pain? Are you painting or fishing? What are you doing with your free time?

Physical

How are you physically? Do you exercise routinely, jog, run marathons? How is your health? Do you have any disabilities? If so, how are you dealing with them? Are you full of energy, life, and enthusiasm as you greet each day? Are you eating well? Are you at your ideal weight?

These are all examples of the types of things to think about and address as you go through this most crucial step. Your mental vision of your ideal Brutally Honest Target Zones should be your own personal vision of the future.

Step Three:

Next, create a symbol and a word (one word only) that you see appearing above the mental picture you created in you mind in step two. See the words and the symbol being crystal clear. You will write the word you created under the symbol. Keep in mind that the symbol you create does not have to be a picture of your mental image. It can be anything—as simple as a star or asterisk or as complex as anything

Brutally Honest Life Management Journal

your mind can create. Be imaginative, and try to create something unique.

Step Four:

Once you have created this very clear vision in your head, say out loud the word that you came up with while still visualizing the picture, symbol, and word. Repeat this ten times as loud as you can—assuming you can do so without your family or friends calling the people in the white jackets to take you away. Say the words with passion. Feel each word as you say it. Clench one of your fists and hit the opposite palm each time you emphatically say the word. The more passionate you are at the time you are thinking of the mental image, the stronger the Power Link. Remember that this is not about conforming to societal expectations. Are you doing something different? Are you doing something that others would look at you oddly for? You bet! You *are* different. The difference is that *you* are choosing excellence.

Understand that as you evolve up the Brutally Honest Success Pathway, there *will* be others who will try to knock you off your path. These Brutally Honest Detractors will try to erode your focus in many different ways. They will laugh at you, chastise you, and make fun of you in any number of disempowering ways. They are a virus that, if left unchecked, can spread to your reticular activating system, spreading negativity throughout. Why do they do this?

While there are many reasons, one of the most significant is their internal barometers, which people use to compare themselves to the rest of the world. There will be people in your life who will be friendly with you as long as you don't exceed where they are in life. They create there own level of success, and each step you take past their stage of life will be met with all of the negativity mentioned above. Most of this is fueled by jealousy, greed, and envy. There will also be people in your life who are genuinely happy and supportive of your success. These individuals, your Brutally Honest Support Squad are the ones you should, and must, seek out. They will supply additional fuel to assist you in your journey. They will support you when you need additional help, encouragement, and ideas. These like-minded individuals will form a team that assists its members in attaining their respective goals because the collective power of the group exceeds the individual capacities of the people within it.

Therefore, knowing that your life will be filled with both types of people, Brutally Honest Detractors and Brutally Honest Support Squad members, you need to eliminate the viruses and add to the Support Squad. Forming a group of like-minded individuals will exponentially increase your chances of success. Have fun with it. Set up monthly Brutally Honest meetings where each member of the group can help the others attain their next levels. Use this journal as a template for the meetings by having each member complete the exercises and use them in each meeting as starting points for discussion. Initial meetings may focus on the creation of ten-year Brutally Honest Target Zones, with each successive meeting evolving through the rest of the journal. The power of the group will serve to provide accountability, keeping members on track, as well as providing additional resources to both assist and move the members forward. You will find that it is incredibly comforting to hear that other members have also felt the same way as you at times.

Step Five:

Put down your journal and move on with the other activities of your day. Sometime later in the day, pull out your journal and look only at the symbols and words you created in step three for each of your Target Zones. If this instantly brings you back to the mental images you created in step two, congratulations! You have now successfully created your Brutally Honest Power Links for your Brutally Honest Target Zones. The seeds of success have been planted.

Now it's your turn. Let's go for it!

Jim

Once again I had missed the wave I was going after, and my surfboard had turned into a giant hunk of foam and fiberglass, looking to take off my head unless I dived for the bottom. Surfing can look so easy from the beach, but as any surfer will tell you, when you add good old Mother Nature into the equation, all bets are off.

At the tender age of thirty-eight, I had received a surfboard for my birthday from my dear wife, Cyndii. I saw her beaming from ear to ear as she walked through the door with this strange object. She was the surfer of the family, and I guess she figured it was time for me to learn. But, while I loved the ocean, I was also a product of the *Jaws* era and stayed comfortably near the shore. (How I overcame that fear is a book in itself.) In any event, I graciously accepted the gift and began to learn how to ride the thing. At the very least, being a surfer was cool.

After three years I sucked and had caught about three waves that I actually stood up on. Then my surfing buddy, Kevin (better known as Krohe), told me about visualization. He said you had to visualize catching the wave and popping up—it was just that simple. As I looked at Krohe, I thought he was nuts. The

Brutally Honest Life Management Journal

> reason he could surf was not visualization, but rather the fact that he had learned to surf as he was learning to walk. Further, he had surfed around the world and even contemplated turning professional.
>
> I thought more about what he had said, and I decided to do some reading about visualization. I found that athletes use this technique to achieve amazing results. The more I thought about it, the more I realized that visualization was an extension of creating a compelling plan and *seeing* it come to life. So I went to bed every night visualizing myself paddling into and catching waves. Every night I saw myself putting together the necessary steps to catching and riding waves.
>
> The next time I went surfing, I actually caught waves (not many, but some!), and my wingman, Stevo, asked me what had changed. I told him what Krohe had said and how I was visualizing myself catching the waves and surfing down the face. Today, I can catch waves and surf. I am just an okay surfer at best, but I have as much fun as anyone. That is how I earned my nickname from the Hatteras Crew—KING GROM! (Grom is short for Grommet or young surfer) I cherish that name, and visualization helped me get it. Please make sure you really focus and visualize your future.

Target Zone 1: _____

Step One:
Complete the statement below.
I will achieve this Target Zone because:

_____
_____
_____
_____
_____

Step Two:
    Close your eyes and create your mental vision of what it will look like when you achieve this Brutally Honest Target Zone.

Step Three:
Draw a symbol to describe this mental picture.

My one word to describe my mental image is_____.

Step Four:
    Say out loud the word that you came up with above, while still visualizing the picture, symbol, and word. Repeat this ten times as loud as you can and with passion. Energize your entire body as you do this.

Step Five:
    Put down the journal and move on with your other activities of the day. Sometime later in the day, pull out your journal and look only at the symbol and word you created in step three. If this instantly brings you back to the mental image you created in step two, congratulations! You have now successfully created your Brutally Honest Power Link for this Brutally Honest Target Zone. The seeds of success have been planted.

Target Zone 2: _____

Step One:
Complete the statement below.
I will achieve this Target Zone because:
_____
_____
_____
_____
_____

Brutally Honest Life Management Journal

Step Two:
Close your eyes and create your mental vision of what it will look like when you achieve this Brutally Honest Target Zone.

Step Three:

Draw a symbol to describe this mental picture.

My one word to describe my mental image is_____.

Step Four:
    Say out loud the word that you came up with above, while still visualizing the picture, symbol, and word. Repeat this ten times as loud as you can and with passion. Energize your entire body as you do this.

Step Five:
    Put down the journal and move on with the other activities of your day. Sometime later in the day, pull out your journal and look only at the symbol and word you created in step three. If this instantly brings you back to the mental image you created in step two, congratulations! You have now successfully created your Brutally Honest Power Link for this Brutally Honest Target Zone. The seeds of success have been planted.

Target Zone 3: _____

Step One:
Complete the statement below.
I will achieve this Target Zone because:

_____

_____

_____

_____

Step Two:

Close your eyes and create your mental vision of what it will look like when you achieve this Brutally Honest Target Zone.

Step Three:

Draw a symbol to describe this mental picture.

My one word to describe my mental image is_____.

Step Four:

Say out loud the word that you came up with above, while still visualizing the picture, symbol, and word. Repeat this ten times as loud as you can and with passion. Energize your entire body as you do this.

Step Five:

Put down the journal and move on with the other activities of your day. Sometime later in the day, pull out your journal and look only at the symbol and word you created in step three. If this instantly brings you back to the mental image you created in step two, congratulations! You have now successfully created your Brutally Honest Power Link for this Brutally Honest Target Zone. The seeds of success have been planted.

Target Zone 4: _____

Brutally Honest Life Management Journal

Step One:
Complete the statement below.
I will achieve this Target Zone because:
_____
_____
_____
_____

Step Two:
Close your eyes and create your mental vision of what it will look like when you achieve this Brutally Honest Target Zone.

Step Three:
Draw a symbol to describe this mental picture.

My one word to describe my mental image is_____.

Step Four:
 Say out loud the word that you came up with above, while still visualizing the picture, symbol, and word. Repeat this ten times as loud as you can and with passion. Energize your entire body as you do this.

Step Five:
 Put down the journal and move on with the other activities of your day. Sometime later in the day, pull out your journal and look only at the symbol and word you created in step three. If this instantly brings you back to the mental image you created in step two, congratulations! You have now successfully created your Brutally Honest Power Link for this Brutally Honest Target Zone. The seeds of success have been planted.

Target Zone 5: _____

Step One:
Complete the statement below.
I will achieve this Target Zone because:

_____
_____
_____
_____

Step Two:
Close your eyes and create your mental vision of what it will look like when you achieve this Brutally Honest Target Zone.

Step Three:
Draw a symbol to describe this mental picture.

My one word to describe my mental image is_____.

Step Four:
Say out loud the word that you came up with above, while still visualizing the picture, symbol, and word. Repeat this ten times as loud as you can and with passion. Energize your entire body as you do this.

Step Five:
Put down the journal and move on with the other activities of your day. Sometime later in the day, pull out your journal and look only at the symbol and word you created in step three. If this instantly brings you back to the mental image you created in step two, congratulations! You have now successfully created your Brutally Honest Power Link for this Brutally Honest Target Zone. The seeds of success have been planted.

Excellent! You have now created a Brutally Honest Power Link to assist you in achieving each of your five Brutally Honest Target Zones. As such, you have just added five more tools to your Brutally Honest Toolbox Of course, even though you are currently focusing on five Brutally Honest Target Zones, this exercise can be used to create as many other Power Links as you want.

> *Nearly all men can stand adversity, but if you want to test a man's character, give him power.*
> —Abraham Lincoln

Your Brutally Honest Power Card

Having successfully powered through all of the lessons we learned along the way, your reticular activating system is now on high alert and programmed for success as it guides you toward the attainment of your Brutally Honest Target Zones. To assist you even further, we will create a Brutally Honest Power Card to keep with you as you venture forth. This Power Card will be *your* unique summary that you will carry with you in your wallet, pocketbook, or any other place that will serve as a reminder. You will initially look at it each morning and before you go to bed.

To create your personalized Power Card, find a small index card, and on one side list each of your five Brutally Honest Target Zones. Next to each, draw the symbol and word you created to represent it. On the back, list all of the Brutally Honest tools that are in your Brutally Honest Toolbox. Write a one-sentence Brutally Honest Power Affirmation on the back that sums up why you are absolutely committed to achieving all of your Brutally Honest Target Zones.

(Front of Card)

BRUTALLY HONEST POWER CARD

Brutally Honest Target Zones

Target Zone 1 Word: Symbol:

Target Zone 2 Word: Symbol:

Target Zone 3 Word: Symbol:

Target Zone 4 Word: Symbol:

Target Zone 5 Word: Symbol:

(Back of Card)

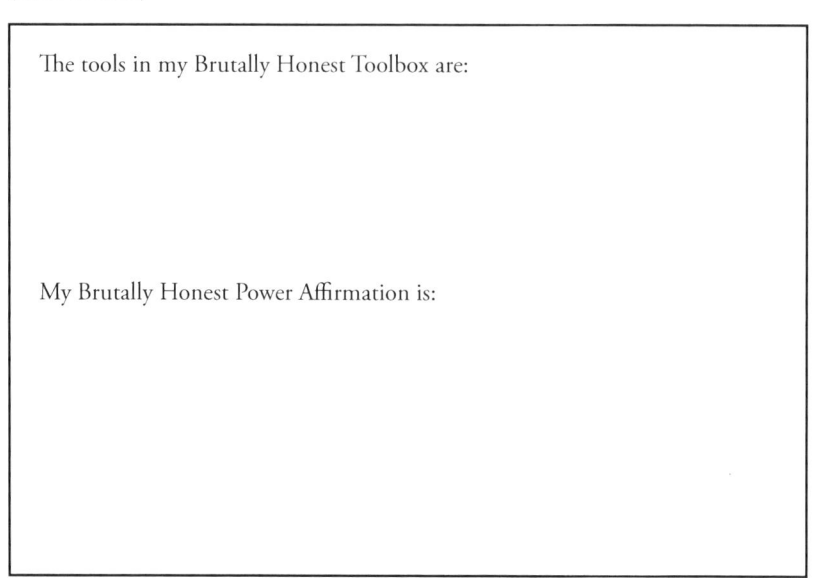

The tools in my Brutally Honest Toolbox are:

My Brutally Honest Power Affirmation is:

Great job! Do you realize that the index card you now hold in your hands is the sum of all of the work you have done thus far. This may be hard to grasp. How can everything you have done in the hundreds of pages of your journal be contained in this tiny card? The question lies in what you have come to know. Through all of your hard work and effort throughout your journey you have programmed—then supercharged—your reticular activating system to be on high alert and to keep you on course to achieve all of your Brutally Honest Target Zones. That said, just like the world's greatest athletes can't peak all of the time and need coaching, your Brutally Honest Power Card will be *your* daily reminder to your reticular activating system to keep you in a peak state—fully engaged.

> *Empowerment is a virtue that is not restricted by age, gender, or social status. Instead, it is available to anyone, at any time, who seeks out this most attainable gift.*
> —Greg LaMonaca

The Brutally Honest Daily Journal: The Final Frontier

A Note from Your Soul

I am extremely proud of you. As your soul and your coach, I have seen you transcend into being an empowered, relentless, focused individual. Your future is now. Your path has been set, and it is made up of invincible bricks. Your destiny is *yours*. You have graduated from BHU (Brutally Honest University) with distinctive honors.

To reward you, I am going to share with you the most empowering and powerful tool. This gift is yours to be added to your Brutally Honest Toolbox. What is this most powerful tool? It's your Brutally Honest Daily Journal. You may be thinking, *Isn't that what I have just done in this journal?* No. What you have done thus far is condition yourself for the next level. The next level of Brutally Honest University is the furtherance of your education to obtain your Brutally Honest Masters Degree, your MBA (Management Based upon taking Action).

In obtaining your undergraduate degree, you took the journey to find me, your soul. Once we were united, I became your coach and held your hand through the process of defining and creating your Brutally Honest Target Zones. It's now time for us to continue our journey as we walk down life's path. As I have been there for you thus far, I pledge my never-ending support to continue to be right there next to you. I am *always* here. You can count on me to answer your questions, give you unconditional support, confidence, and encouragement.

During our undergraduate days, you learned the importance of *writing down* all of your information, as you have done throughout this journal. You learned that by physically committing your thoughts and feelings to writing, you have exponentially increased the chances of success. With each stroke of your pen or pencil you have created another layer to your reticular activating system, supercharging it to seek out your Brutally Honest Target Zones. Not only have you written throughout, but you have also *repeatedly* written out your Brutally Honest Target Zones. This told your reticular activating system to be especially on the lookout for these highlighted items.

It would follow then that each and every time you commit things to writing, your chances of ongoing success increase. Your Brutally Honest Daily Journal will be your direct connection with me as you forge forward. The rules are the same for your

Brutally Honest Life Management Journal

Brutally Honest Daily Journal as they were for this journal. It's for your eyes only. No rules, no grades, and no judgment. It should be a personal chronology of your life. Your thoughts, concerns, ideas, how your day went, what you learned, what you did right, what you did wrong. As always, it is essential that you are Brutally Honest as you make your daily entries.

Your Brutally Honest Daily Journal will also be the place where you track the progress of your Brutally Honest Target Zones at periodic intervals. You must honestly assess how you are doing. If you only write what is going right, you will never transcend into the elite group of super achievers.

Your journal is also a place where you plan your life by assessing what is going on and what *possibilities and opportunities* are present. Recently, we have been living through one of the worst economic times in U.S. history since the Great Depression. We have undergone severe financial strife. Countless jobs have been lost; trillions of dollars have evaporated from the stock market; uncertainty and fear are at all-time highs; people are losing homes at record levels as foreclosures are rampant. Families are trying to figure out where there next meals are coming from. While the government has attempted to assist, its efforts have thus far come up short as we have fallen further and further. Gloom and doom has been everywhere … or has it? No doubt this is an unprecedented time with many dire consequences. That said, you basically have two choices: be depressed and focus on everything that is going wrong and why your life is miserable without hope or focus on what is going right. Has this situation brought you and your family closer together? Have you developed better saving habits? Have you stayed committed to your dollar-cost-averaging investment strategy and bought quality blue-chip company stock at bargain prices? Have you invested in real estate, which is at an all-time low? Have you spent more time playing board games with your family and friends instead of going out to dinner? Have you mentored someone younger than you on how to be a better person? Is your vision for the future compelling and full of hope? Are you using the problems as lessons on what to avoid in the future?

Where there are problems, there are also opportunities—but only if you are willing to look for them. If you focus on only what is going wrong, you will continue to be depressed. Use every negative situation as an opportunity to learn, to grow, and to pick out the diamonds in the rough. Your journal is your tool for finding these things.

Ideally, your Brutally Honest Daily Journal should be just that, a daily journal. I realize that there will be periods during which you will be unable to keep this daily commitment. However, know that with each entry, your chances of success increase. Your journal should contain weekly, monthly, semi-annual, and yearly summaries. You will find that it will be your tool to help you through the occasional stumbling blocks as you can go to previous entries in which you addressed being confronted with similar obstacles and analyze how you got through them and dealt with them.

You will feel empowered each time you look back into the earlier entries as you see your progress in black and white. It is at these moments that seeds of empowerment grow in abundance. Until then you will have only dealt with future targets. While you will have visualized these moments, they would previously only have been visions. When you actually see *your* visions becoming reality, you will have an overwhelming sense of accomplishment. It will create a warm shower of endorphins that rains down over your reticular activating system, causing it to engage its highest level of alert, which will create a drive in you that is unparalleled. When these moments occur—and they *will* occur—detail them in your journal. Be vivid, colorful, and passionate.

Most important, as you reach each of your Brutally Honest Target Zones, take time to celebrate your accomplishments. Reward yourself in some way—maybe with a dinner, a trip, or perhaps a weekend of doing nothing. Whatever you choose, make it rewarding.

We have not spent all of this time creating your Brutally Honest Target Zones so you can simply achieve them and forget about them. You must let your reticular activating system know that these moments, these accomplishments that you focused on many months or years ago have arrived and that they are as wonderful as the visions that created them. It's a way of saying thank you to your reticular activating system for guiding you toward their attainment.

Life is not about creating a checklist of to-do's and moving down a conveyer belt to check off those things that we have accomplished. The reason we painstakingly created our Brutally Honest Target Zones was to develop those powerful, important, and select areas that were most important to us in order to create a fulfilling and rewarding life. Each of these amazing milestones must be recognized and rewarded. Taking time to enjoy the present is as important as defining and creating a compelling future.

Lastly, should you choose, your Brutally Honest daily journal will form a lasting legacy for your children, relatives, and significant others. Can you think of any greater gift to give your children than a journal containing a lifetime of lessons?

Soul Mates for Life

I have said a lot throughout our journey together. As your soul, I have been your coach, mentor, friend, and fan. It is now time for you to speak. It's your time to go forward into the world, embracing all of life's beauty and possibilities. Your chance to make an indelible mark on this world. Everything you do, every breath you take, every action, good or bad, creates ripples. Like a stone hitting a calm lake, the ripples go off into infinity.

- What ripples will you make?
- Will you simply put this journal on a bookshelf, or will you reread it and refer to it often?
- Will you actively keep and maintain your Brutally Honest daily journal, or will you revert back to simply wishing or hoping?
- Will you be the person who makes a difference in the world, or will you simply be the one who reads about those who do?
- Will you continually say that you will take action tomorrow, next week, next month, or will you take immediate action today?

The answers lie in your commitment. Having reached this point, you are now a member of the Brutally Honest Power Elite—a highly unique, special, and elite group of individuals who have committed to taking action, being personally accountable, and doing whatever it takes to achieve, a group of individuals who are committed to excellence and are joined together by this common bond.

As your partner throughout this journey, I have known the answer to all of the questions above all along. *You will succeed.* How do I know this? Because you are *already* successful. You are *already* a winner. It is with these distinctions that I am confident in your attainment of your Brutally Honest Target Zones and *anything* else you commit yourself to doing.

As we end this stage of our life together, it is important to know that although we have set ten-year targets, God willing, life will not end in ten years. Life is an ever unfolding amazing journey full of hope and adventure. We must constantly monitor, evaluate, reevaluate, modify, correct, and—if necessary—change our path. Because of circumstances that arise, both good and bad, we may need to change our Brutally Honest Target Zones. You must also create new Brutally Honest Target Zones at periodic intervals to create new success pathways into your future. You should continually revisit this journal and periodically go through the process again. Make sure you also diligently utilize your Brutally Honest daily journal each day if possible.

Lastly, give back and share what you have learned with as many others as will listen. Teaching others reinforces the lessons you have learned and, more important, touches their lives so that they too can be empowered and subsequently teach and touch others lives, continuing the positive ripples that you started, which will solidify your mark on this world. Thank you for engaging me and allowing me to be a part of your life. I am here for you, your soul mate for life.

> *When you have decided what you believe, what you feel must be done, have the courage to stand alone and be counted.*
> —Eleanor Roosevelt

> *You will know when you have found your Soul's Core when you are comfortable with* who you are, what you are, *and* where you are going. *You will truly have learned from your past and will be living in the present and planning for your awesome future. STAY STOKED*
> —James H. Grim Jr. t

About the Authors

Gregory P. LaMonaca, Esq.

Gregory P. LaMonaca, Esq., husband and father, is the founder of the Law Office of Gregory P. LaMonaca, P.C., who has been selected on multiple occasions to both Philadelphia Magazine and Mail Line Today magazine's top Lawyer edition's, a former martial arts instructor, and owner of several other businesses including the Creative Venture Group and co-founder of the Brutally Honest Company.

James H. Grim Jr.

James H. Grim Jr., husband and father, is a graduate of Capitol College and Pennsylvania State University, where he obtained his bachelors and masters degrees, respectively, in engineering. Mr. Grim worked for General Electric and for Ulticom, where he helped initiate a successful initial public offering. In pursuit of his entrepreneurial passion, Mr. Grim purchased Ultimate Image Salon, Inc., created Ultimate Salon Consulting and co-founded the Brutally Honest Company.

Index

Symbols

5 years 49, 90, 91, 92, 94, 96, 98, 103, 106, 107, 110
5-Year Target 94
10 years 69, 70, 73, 76, 79, 80, 81, 82, 83, 84, 85, 87, 90, 118, 123, 127, 132, 137, 193

A

adaptation xxii, 86, 90, 142, 144
Alyssa ix, xxviii, xxxi, xxxiii, xxxv, xxxviii, xxxix, xl
anchor 65, 153
anger 145, 171
A Note on Discipline 64
Anthony Robbins xxv, 118
anxiety 96
attitude xxix, xxx, xxxii, xxxvi, xxxviii, 22, 61, 88, 136
auditory 19

B

batteries 26, 28, 29, 30, 31, 32, 33, 34, 35, 36, 37, 39, 41, 43, 45, 47, 49, 50, 52, 54, 56
beliefs 7, 22, 61, 78
belief system 78
Better health xxv
Blasting Off to Utopia 78
bliss 144
Breakdown xxi, xxii, xxiii, 1, 2, 62, 67, 69, 87
Brian's Song 146
Brother Bear 157, 158
Brutally Honest Bank Account 86, 87, 89
Brutally Honest board of directors 91, 92
Brutally Honest Bridge 90
Brutally Honest coach 62
Brutally Honest Daily Journal 189, 190
Brutally Honest Detractors 178
Brutally Honest Emotional Volcano 147, 148, 149, 150
Brutally Honest Empowerment Zone 144
Brutally Honest Filters 146
Brutally Honest Free Flow 70, 72
Brutally Honest Inventory 17
Brutally Honest Life Management System xxi, 76
Brutally Honest Masters Degree 189
Brutally Honest Net Life Statement 96
Brutally Honest Net Worth statement 87
Brutally Honest Power Affirmation 187, 188
Brutally Honest Power Card 187
Brutally Honest Power Elite 192
Brutally Honest Power Link 175, 181, 182, 183, 184, 185
Brutally Honest Success Pathway 78, 79, 87, 90, 92, 114, 120, 144, 178
Brutally Honest Support Squad 178
Brutally Honest Target Zones xvii, xxi, xxv, 27, 67, 68, 72, 73, 74, 75, 76, 78, 79, 80, 85, 86, 89, 90, 92, 114, 115, 116, 117, 118, 120, 141, 142, 143, 144, 145, 146, 152, 154, 156, 160, 161, 170, 173, 175, 177, 179, 185, 186, 187, 188, 189, 190, 191, 192, 193
Brutally Honest Toolbox 144, 145, 151, 155, 185, 187, 188, 189
Brutally Honest Tools 144, 175, 187
Brutally Honest University 189
Brutally Honest Veil of Comfort 118, 120
Brutally Honest versus the Gurus 22

C

calculated risk 116
Caraline v, ix
career xxv, 27, 64, 69, 72, 177
categories xi, 23, 28, 72, 73, 74, 75, 76, 78, 79, 151
certainty xxv, 76, 117
clarity 61, 62, 67, 75, 89, 147
coach 62, 63, 69, 76, 78, 85, 91, 151, 189, 192
conditioning xxxvi, 16, 23, 67, 86, 144, 167, 173
conversation with your soul 1
Core xxi, 2, 23, 24, 28, 56, 60, 61, 62, 69, 75, 146, 192
creativity 157, 158
Cyndii v, ix, 179

D

depression xvii, xxiii, 17, 145, 171, 190
disappointment 10
discipline 64
Disneyland xxiv, 143

E

elation 145, 171
embarrassment 3, 35, 56
emotional states 146, 151
emotional tool 155, 156
empathy 146, 167
empowered 1, 62, 114, 151, 189, 191, 193
engage your soul 67
envy 56, 178
excitement 10, 62

F

failures xvi, xx, 85, 88, 120
family ix, x, xix, xxi, xxiv, xxxii, xxxiii, xl, xli, 6, 22, 24, 25, 27, 28, 29, 31, 33, 36, 37, 39, 41, 42, 43, 50, 56, 59, 61, 69, 73, 76, 79, 80, 85, 92, 115, 144, 175, 176, 178, 179, 190
Family Members Who Drain Our Batteries 36
father xix, xxxviii, 3, 4, 5, 36, 60, 68, 115, 168, 169, 195
fear xxv, 145, 171
finances 69, 72, 73, 91, 176
focus xxxiv, xli, 1, 19, 24, 27, 33, 34, 61, 62, 67, 75, 76, 80, 91, 92, 117, 118, 144, 145, 146, 155, 173, 178, 179, 180, 190
Free Flow 70, 72, 78
Friday the 13th 146
Friends 43, 176
Friends Who Drain Our Batteries 43
frustration 145, 171
fulfilling career xxv
full immersion xvi, 1
funnel 115

G

goals xix, xxi, xxii, xxiv, 23, 68, 72, 87
GPS 75
great marriage xxiv
greed 56, 178
Gregory iv, ix, xx, xxii, xxvii, xxxi, xxxiii, xxxv, xxxviii, xxxix, xl, 17, 38, 61, 78, 85, 87, 93, 142, 195
Gustatory 19

H

happiness xx, xxv, 2, 23, 26
health xi, xxiv, xxv, xxvii, xxix, xxx, 27, 69, 72, 86, 92, 176, 177
healthy life xxiv
heart x, xxxiii, 22, 26, 60, 65, 70, 168
hobbies 25, 69, 176
honesty 64, 145, 171

I

individuals xiii, xv, xvi, xvii, xxi, xxxi, 11, 14, 19, 25, 27, 28, 29, 30,

31, 32, 35, 36, 37, 56, 117, 145, 178, 192
integrity 145, 171
Investment properties xxv

J

James H. Grim Jr iv, 192, 195
jealousy 145, 171
job xxiii, xxxviii, xxxix, 7, 55, 82, 85, 91, 92, 188
journal xv, xvi, xvii, xviii, xix, xxi, xxii, xxvii, xxix, xli, 4, 33, 56, 66, 90, 118, 143, 144, 157, 179, 181, 182, 183, 184, 185, 188, 189, 190, 191, 192, 193
joy xiii, xxxiii, 82

K

Kinesthetic 19

L

large family xxiv
laser-beam focus 146
Letter to Your Soul 1
leverage 59, 60, 96, 97, 101, 105, 109, 113, 120, 122, 126, 130, 134, 139
Life Management Journal i, iii, ix, xv
Longwood Gardens 168
loss of weight xxiii, 17

M

Meghan v, ix, 12
millionaire 61, 68, 73
momentum 118, 120, 142
Monica ix, xxviii, xxxi, xxxiii, xxxiv, xxxv, xxxvii, xxxviii, xxxix, xl, 22, 25
mother xix, xxiii, 5, 6, 9, 12, 60, 168, 169

N

negative xxxi, 26, 28, 36, 56, 59, 65, 66, 87, 90, 96, 145, 146, 147, 151, 152, 153, 154, 157, 167, 168, 170, 171, 172, 173, 175, 190
negative emotion 170, 173
negative states 145, 170, 171, 172, 175
Net Life Statement 28, 62, 73, 96
Net Worth 87

O

obstacles xvi, xxi, xxxi, xxxiii, 22, 25, 86, 91, 95, 96, 99, 100, 104, 108, 111, 112, 115, 120, 124, 125, 129, 133, 138, 191
Olfactory 19
one-year target 115, 120, 121, 124, 125, 129, 133, 138
outcomes 75, 79, 80, 81, 82, 83, 84, 85, 89, 117

P

pain xxvii, xxviii, xxix, xxx, xxxiii, xxxiv, xxxvii, xxxix, xl, 3, 9, 10, 37, 38, 40, 41, 44, 45, 46, 47, 50, 51, 52, 54, 56, 57, 58, 59, 60, 93, 136, 169, 170, 177
painful xvi, xxxvi, xxxviii, 1, 3, 9, 10, 12, 13, 14, 15, 35, 169
parents xix, xxiv, xxx, 3, 4, 22, 25, 73, 76, 79, 80, 89, 90, 168
passion xix, xxi, 195
past xv, xvi, xx, xxv, xxix, xxxv, 4, 9, 12, 13, 14, 15, 16, 22, 28, 35, 37, 38, 43, 49, 50, 61, 62, 69, 72, 76, 87, 88, 89, 90, 116, 118, 142, 143, 144, 145, 177, 178, 192
patterns xvii, 37, 152, 154, 156
perception 61, 68
physiology 10, 13
pleasure ix, 12, 19, 86, 98, 168

positive xxi, xxxii, xxxvii, xli, 1, 13, 19, 24, 25, 26, 27, 28, 60, 65, 66, 87, 91, 136, 145, 146, 147, 151, 154, 155, 156, 157, 158, 161, 167, 168, 170, 171, 172, 173, 175, 193
positive emotion 157, 170, 173
positive states 145, 170, 171, 172, 173
Power Link 175, 178, 181, 182, 183, 184, 185
Power Statement 123, 127, 131, 136, 141

Q

quest xxiv, 72, 120, 142
Quest for Utopia 142

R

reality xvi, xviii, xxii, xxiv, 17, 61, 67, 70, 72, 82, 85, 87, 89, 116, 142, 160, 191
recondition 67
Reticular Activating System (RAS) 75, 90, 91, 116, 117, 144, 145, 146, 153, 154, 157, 158, 167, 169, 173, 178, 187, 188, 189, 191
ripples 192, 193

S

self-analysis xxii, 37, 43, 50
self-esteem 33
self-help xxi, xxii, xxiii, 17, 61, 72, 89
society xx, xxi, 1, 2, 56, 62, 67
Soul Mates for Life 192
Soul's Core xxi, 2, 23, 24, 28, 61, 62, 69, 146, 192
subcategories 73
subsist 85
success bricks 87
success seeds xx, 85
supercharge 29, 30, 31, 32, 34, 66, 69, 118
Supercharging Your Batteries 25

T

target xvii, xxi, xxv, 27, 63, 67, 68, 72, 73, 74, 75, 76, 78, 79, 80, 81, 82, 83, 84, 85, 86, 89, 90, 91, 92, 94, 98, 102, 103, 106, 110, 114, 115, 116, 117, 118, 119, 120, 121, 123, 127, 131, 132, 136, 137, 141, 142, 143, 144, 145, 146, 152, 154, 156, 160, 161, 162, 163, 164, 170, 173, 175, 176, 177, 179, 180, 181, 182, 183, 184, 185, 186, 187, 188, 189, 190, 191, 192, 193
Target Zones xvii, xxi, xxv, 27, 63, 67, 68, 72, 73, 74, 75, 76, 78, 79, 80, 85, 86, 89, 90, 91, 92, 94, 114, 115, 116, 117, 118, 120, 141, 142, 143, 144, 145, 146, 152, 154, 156, 160, 161, 170, 173, 175, 177, 179, 185, 186, 187, 188, 189, 190, 191, 192, 193
Tasha ix, 157, 158
the Breakdown Phase xxi, 1, 2, 67, 87
The Law of Attraction 19, 72
The Negative Drain on Our Batteries 35
The Painful Past 9
The Past xx, xxv, xxix, 28, 35, 37, 38, 43, 50, 61, 62, 88, 89, 116, 144
The Pleasant Past 12
The Present 17, 24, 56, 91, 96, 143, 191, 192
things xiii, xvii, xviii, xix, xx, xxii, xxiv, xxvii, xxx, xxxi, xxxii, xxxiii, xxxiv, xxxv, xxxvi, xxxvii, xxxviii, xxxix, xli, 1, 2, 4, 5, 7, 9, 10, 13, 15, 19, 22, 23, 24, 25, 26, 28, 29, 30, 31, 32, 33, 34, 35, 36, 37, 43, 56, 57, 59, 61, 62, 63, 65, 66, 69, 70, 76, 78, 79, 80, 86, 89, 92, 94, 95, 96, 97, 98, 100, 101, 103, 104, 105, 107, 108, 109, 110, 112, 113, 114,

116, 119, 120, 122, 123, 125, 126, 128, 129, 130, 132, 133, 134, 137, 138, 139, 142, 143, 144, 152, 158, 167, 168, 170, 176, 177, 189, 190, 191
Things in Life That Charge Our Batteries 33
Things in Life That Drain Our Batteries 56
time-management 72
Tony and Sarah 167, 170
triggers 35, 37, 43, 50, 153, 173

U

uncertainty 76, 116, 190
Utopia xviii, xxi, xxii, 76, 78, 142

V

vision xvi, xx, 4, 26, 68, 70, 72, 73, 75, 76, 79, 85, 90, 115, 143, 176, 177, 178, 180, 182, 183, 184, 185, 190
visual 19

W

wealth and prosperity xxv
work iv, ix, xviii, xxi, xxiii, xxiv, xxviii, xxix, xxxi, xxxii, xxxiii, xxxiv, xxxvi, 2, 9, 24, 25, 26, 28, 30, 31, 35, 49, 50, 52, 54, 61, 64, 72, 115, 142, 152, 158, 173, 176, 177, 188
Work Associates Who Drain Our Batteries 49
worry 3, 96

Z

Zone of Comfort 116, 117
Zone of Excellence 115, 116, 117

Made in the USA
Middletown, DE
17 February 2017